YOUR
LIFE
INSURANCE

THE DREYFUS FAMILY MONEY MANAGEMENT SERVICE

MAKING YOUR LIFE INSURANCE WORK FOR YOU

by SAL NUCCIO
and the Editors of Dreyfus Publications

illustrated by Roy Doty

DREYFUS PUBLICATIONS LTD.   NEW YORK

SAL NUCCIO, administrative vice-president of a group of insurance and financial service companies, doubles in brass as a free-lance writer in the field of finance. Previously he was on the staff of "The New York Times" as a financial columnist and investigative reporter. While there he originated the "Personal Finance" column of the paper. He is the author of "The New York Times Guide to Personal Finance," published by Harper & Row in 1967.

THE DREYFUS FAMILY MONEY MANAGEMENT SERVICE

Jay Gold
EDITORIAL DIRECTOR

Sandylee Williams
EDITORIAL ASSISTANT

Spero Yianilos
ASSISTANT EDITOR

John M. Hix
ART CONSULTANT

DREYFUS PUBLICATIONS LTD.

Jerome S. Hardy
PRESIDENT

George Erikson
LEGAL DEPARTMENT

Heinz Eller
EXECUTIVE VICE-PRESIDENT

Robert F. Dubuss
Julian Smerling
FINANCIAL DEPARTMENT

Sally J. Reich
Martin Stone
VICE-PRESIDENTS

Arlene Armstrong
BUSINESS OFFICE

CONTENTS

A NOTE TO THE READER

This book, like its companion volumes in this series, has been planned to be as functional as it is informative. For that reason, the typographic design for the text specifies exceptionally wide margins. These are meant to be used for anything that will be helpful to you: for notetaking, reminders to yourself or even doing arithmetical calculations. The editors hope you will find the margins useful.

The stock for these books was selected in part because it can be written on equally well with pencil, or ballpoint or felt-tipped pen.

The colored rules you will find scattered throughout the book are used to emphasize salient portions of the text.

—— THE EDITORS

A question that is a crucial part of a bigger question on your life-insurance program is this: how much are you depending on life insurance as death protection and how much as savings and/or investment?

CHAPTER I

How Much
Is Enough?

Bill was doing quite well for himself. Without being complacent, he was pleased with his life thus far. At 30, he had been married for eight years to his college sweetheart, Grace. They had two attractive and healthy children.

He was earning a good income in a career job he enjoyed, and he and Grace had plans. They were going to do things for the kids, and for themselves. While not all of their plans required money, a good many of them did. But Bill and his wife were not worried. He was earning $15,000 a year, with the promise of more as he won advancement. They had come a long way from their early years of struggle.

The supply of life insurance—and the
kinds, too—may seem limitless.
But it makes no sense to buy more than is right for you.

Being a sensible couple, they realized that life isn't all roses. So they kept a small savings account to meet emergencies, and Bill carried a comprehensive family accident and health insurance plan as a fringe benefit on his job. But they hadn't taken all the steps that would ease the economic pressure of Bill's death. It was just too morbid a subject to discuss.

They recognized, though, that it would be a lot easier to discuss it now, when death seemed so remote, so talk they did. They had as yet not built up sufficient assets of the type that could provide an adequate income for Grace and the children, should Bill die. And Bill was aware, though only vaguely, that Social Security benefits were not adequate either. So he was convinced, he told Grace, that life insurance was their answer. Furthermore, life insurance built cash to help meet their retirement needs, making it a good investment, too. Or so he thought.

Bill had heard somewhere that a man should carry life insurance amounting to four to five times his annual income. In his case, that would mean up to $75,000 of insurance.

He already had coverage of $30,000, through a group policy provided by his employer, and the $5,000 policy he had bought when their first child was born. That meant he would need another $40,000. But that, he found, would cost more than they could afford, particularly with the retirement-cash feature he wanted.

"If we bought that big policy," Grace said, "we'd be skimping so much that it would be as if we put more importance on dying than living. We'd be what they call 'insurance poor' and that wouldn't make any sense. There must be a better way, and we'd better find it."

And they did.

A little library research showed that their basic ideas were reasonably sound, but a little out of focus for lack of information.

First, Bill had looked to life insurance as much for

Premiums for life insurance can exhaust
you, and your funds, too, if you buy
senselessly. You need a plan tailored for you.

retirement benefits as for economic protection against death.

Actually, the primary function of life insurance is the provision of that death protection, and nothing else does the job better. It should be bought with that in mind.

All other features of life insurance—as savings or as an investment or for retirement benefits—are secondary. An astute money manager generally would not be lured by these features, for when taken out of a policy's context they usually do not compare favorably with other savings and investment plans.

When a generalization is not a guide

Retirement benefits can make up part of any person's life-insurance program, but to include those benefits in the total program makes it prohibitively costly and impractical.

Next, Bill learned that there was no simple guide to the question of how much life insurance he needed. The four to five times his annual income, for example, that he had heard about was only one of many generalizations that were invalid.

Life insurance cannot be measured in dollars but in terms of what it must accomplish in a

The first step in programing your life
insurance is to figure out what is
already available, including life insurance.

family estate-planning program. Insurance, together with other resources of the insured and his family, should provide the money the insured's dependents would need upon his death.

Other sources of support may include savings, investments, Social Security benefits, Veterans Administration benefits, and death benefits provided by an employer, a union, a professional association or a fraternal order.

So a life-insurance plan must be tailored to one's

particular needs. It must mesh with many variable personal factors, such as income and other resources, the size of the family, the ages of the children, their health, and one's objectives in life.

The estate plan and the resultant life-insurance program that would come out of Bill's and Grace's analysis of their situation would not suit your needs, just as mine would not suit yours or Bill's. We each have to work out our own highly individualized plans.

Bill discovered he had given short shrift to some important assets; these, when properly evaluated, would provide a substantial foundation for their program. In fact, when he and Grace matched their assets and resources to their ultimate estate plan, they found that there was little more they needed to do at the moment to achieve nominal security.

The major assets that would be available to Grace at Bill's death totaled $48,600 at this time. They were as follows:

Cash savings .... $ 2,500
Securities 3,000
Savings bonds (gifts from the
        children's grandparents) 700
Company profit-sharing fund 2,400
Equity in their house 5,000
Group-life insurance 30,000
Individual life policy 5,000

Assuming that Grace would remain in their house after Bill's death, they reduced the assets by the $5,000 represented by their equity in the house. Now they had $43,600. They then earmarked $8,600 for certain estate-plan components (which we'll come to later), leaving $35,000 to be invested to provide income for Grace and the children. Conservatively invested at 6%, this would produce $2,100 a year, or $175 a month. That income would be too small to be subject to income taxes.

The money he had ignored

On top of that investment income would be the monthly Social Security survivor's benefits, which Bill had largely ignored. As the Social Security law stood in the fall of 1972, these would amount to $527.60, tax-free, for Grace and the two children.

Your life insurance should fit you like a
well tailored suit—but it would
probably not fit anyone else as well.

So there would be a total monthly income of about
$700.

Grace's own Social Security benefits would end
when the youngest child turned 18, but the children
would each continue to receive $219.90 a month

until age 22, if they were full-time students. These ultimate survivors' benefits would increase with each year that Bill worked, and there was reason to expect that over the years Congress would continue to liberalize Social Security payments as it had in the past.

Grace and Bill were considerably more confident when they had completed their planning than they had been at the beginning. Their procedure, once they knew what they were doing, followed classic lines.

In estate planning, a family must determine the long-term and short-term economic needs that would apply in the event the prime income producer dies. The family then must estimate the sufficiency of available resources in filling those needs. The function of life insurance in estate planning is to close the gaps left by those resources.

Once an estate plan has been formulated, the family should immediately fill with life insurance as much of the gap between what is needed and what is already available as sensible budgeting will allow. With the master plan serving as a guide, other insurance needs can be met as the family's income increases. The important thing is to keep the planning flexible, allowing for upward or downward revision as family circumstances change.

The function of life insurance is to
fill up any gap that shows between what there
is and what will be needed.

The major components of an estate plan, taking into consideration all financial resources, are these:

Immediate cash for death expenses: (Some insurance men call this the "clean-up fund.") It would pay the increasingly high cost of dying—medical and funeral expenses, debts, taxes and estate-settlement fees, including that of a lawyer. The medical, hospital and other costs of a final illness or fatal accident could exceed the limits of accident and health insurance coverage. A minimum allocation would be $2,000, and this amount should be increased as a family's circumstances warrant it.

Estate planning calls for precision.

Bill and Grace decided $2,000 would be sufficient for them in immediate cash for death expenses.

• Readjustment fund: Breathing space is needed by a family faced with the psychological and economic problems caused by the death of the father. Important decisions must be made, and making them in haste could prove costly.

Should the house be sold?

Should a family business be sold?

Must the widow or older children seek work, and, if so, would special training be needed?

A family may have to lower its living standards, and the readjustment fund would allow it the time to prepare for that change. Most important, it would free the family from major decisions in a difficult emotional period. Ideally, the fund should equal six months to a year of the husband's after-tax income, minus what would have been his expenses.

Five thousand dollars was the amount Bill and Grace set aside for a readjustment fund, even though they were convinced that only a fraction of that would be needed in their circumstances.

• Mortgage fund: If a family lives in its own home on which there is a mortgage, allowance for full repayment of the mortgage provides the survivors with relatively low-cost housing if they choose to remain in their home. If they decide to sell, elimination of high monthly mortgage payments would relieve the pressure to sell quickly—possibly at a loss. The entire sale price would be available for other needs. Certain low-cost life insurance policies are designed for this purpose, and Bill and Grace chose to buy one.

They took out a policy that cost $5.64 a month. If Bill died the next day, that would pay off the $24,500 mortgage on the house. The amount of insurance protection would decrease as the principal of the mortgage was paid off.

• Family income: An actual budget showing minimal family needs should be drawn up, subject to periodic review. It should be borne in mind that the greatest need for income occurs when the children are young. Once this is done, it should be determined how much of the budget would be covered by existing assets and potential benefits, including Social Security payments and benefits available to many dependent survivors of armed forces veterans.

Insurance proceeds may take the form of a lump-sum payment—that is, immediate cash that could be invested, providing income while preserving the principal. (This is how Grace and Bill planned to use the proceeds of their existing $35,000 of insurance.) Or the benefits may take the form of a monthly income paid by the insurance company.

As we will see, there are family-income plans that may be added to basic policies at relatively small cost, paying a monthly check to a family in the crucial years while the children are growing up.

• Emergency fund: This would meet an unexpected crisis, such as a major illness. Without it, the well planned but perhaps restricted financial program of a widow may be disrupted. About $1,000 would suffice, but the size and health of the family are key factors. Bill insisted on a minimum of $1,600 for this purpose.

• Income for the widow: This would be reduced in proportion to the widow's reduction in financial responsibility to the children. After the children are on their own, she may not need extra income if she has remarried or taken a job. But it must be remembered that the employment market and the income potential for middle-aged women with only nominal experience never has been large.

Between 18 and 60

Her Social Security benefits normally would stop when the youngest child turned 18, and would not resume until she was 60; even then, supplemental income would be most helpful. For this purpose, Bill and Grace allocated the proceeds from the sale of the house after the children were grown. Grace would get the full value, because the mortgage would have been paid off at Bill's death by the special mortgage-redemption policy he had bought.

• Special funds: The objective of these may be to meet future goals, such as paying for college expenses. Of course, fulfillment of goals in this category comes after basic needs have been satisfied. Bill and Grace did nothing about this component of their plan, deciding that when the time came, other assets would help pay for tuition and other costs. One of these assets would be the $35,000 in insurance proceeds invested to provide supplemental income in the early years. Another, if needed, would be the proceeds from the sale of the house. They also hoped that part-time jobs and other resources would help pay the bills.

You should not be discouraged by the magnitude of the estate plan that all these components might suggest. Few families have the assets or the means to buy the life insurance necessary to establish a complete estate program. But the very exercise of formulating a program will stimulate constructive thinking about what can be done to make the family's way easier, should the father die.

Most important: this preparatory thinking and discussion can and should be accomplished now, without the emotional pressure death can exert on a family.

As with Bill and Grace, it often comes as a surprise to a couple that so much can be accomplished. At the very least, a family would have a head start in its new way of life if it can be assured of only three components: immediate cash for death expenses; a readjustment fund; and a mortgage fund.

With these assured, the family can now begin considering what might be done to supplement income or accomplish particular goals. The mother and older children, for example, might think about what type of work they could undertake to increase earnings. The whole family might consider how the children could get through college. They could examine the prospects for scholarships, student loans, part-time jobs.

The very exercise of planning an estate makes clear that life insurance needs generally cannot be met by one round sum. There may be short-term and long-term needs, lump-sum and monthly-payment requirements.

No rule of thumb

It is sometimes recommended that the widow immediately receive the cash proceeds of all insurance policies. But even in this instance the amount would have been established by the components in an estate plan, not by any rule-of-thumb formula. The sum of the cash proceeds of all insurance policies, together with other cash and invested assets, could be invested in sound securities, perhaps high-yield bonds, or a mutual fund stressing income and preservation of capital, or quality stocks. The investment income would be supplemented by Social Security and other benefits. When college or other special projects call for expenditures, a part of the principal could be used.

Under the right circumstances, this plan could be the best approach. But certain factors must be considered: is the widow capable of handling a large sum of money? If not, it may be prearranged that she invest in specific types of bonds or mutual funds, or that she put the funds into the hands of a reputable investment-counseling firm.

Of paramount importance is the principle that no more insurance than necessary be carried at any time. Short-term needs, such as income supplements when the children are young, should be filled with the cheapest life insurance obtainable, and that should steadily reduce and finally expire as the need is reduced and finally ends. So-called permanent policies should be considered only for long-term insurance needs, such as for death expenses and income for the wife in her later years.

Never carry a bigger load than you absolutely have to. Adequate life-insurance coverage is a necessity. But an overabundance of life insurance is wastefully costly and impractical, whether you can afford to pay the premiums or not.

With all of this in mind, Bill and Grace felt considerably reassured about their estate planning. With their assets, current and potential, considerably more than they had at first thought, and their needs not as stringent as they had feared, they concluded that for now all they needed was the insurance that would automatically pay off the mortgage in the event of Bill's untimely death.

CHAPTER II

Where
and How
to Buy

After the function of life insurance in an estate plan has been defined and pin-pointed, as Bill and Grace did in the previous chapter, the next problem is the selection of appropriate policies. A young man or woman might pay as little as $5 a year for $1,000 of protection, or as much as $45, depending on the type of contract involved. If he or she needs a great deal of protection, the most expensive contract won't do because it would be too expensive for, say, $50,000 of protection.

But would the least expensive one be the wise choice?

As Bill and Grace learned from their research efforts, most of the answers, at least in general terms, can be found in reference books and in pertinent articles in consumer-oriented and general magazines and newspapers. Bill and Grace came to realize that a good agent could help to provide the specific answers, and they set about selecting one. The knowledge about life insurance they had accumulated would not only make it possible for them to conduct an intelligent discussion with an agent, it would also make it possible for them to evaluate his usefulness to them as a counselor.

The products of a good life-insurance company are like building blocks for a creative insurance agent to use in putting together a program to satisfy customers' needs within the limits of their budgets.

Choosing an agent, Bill and Grace had read, requires the same kind of care needed in picking a lawyer. If a salesman does not come recommended by respected acquaintances, then he should be able to provide references, and his company should be a sound one. (Any question concerning a company, or any other aspect of insurance, should be put to your state's insurance-regulatory department.)

Not all life-insurance agents are equally good,
or equally good for you. Credentials
and reputation should be carefully investigated.

Grace's mother had asked them to do her other daughter's husband, Jay, a favor by buying their insurance from him. They did not, because they were convinced he was not qualified. As it happened, like a number of others in the business, Jay was selling insurance only "temporarily" until a "better opportunity" came along. Who needed that?

The couple saw two agents who had been recommended to Bill by business associates. Both men were quite capable, but one of them seemed outstanding.

However, by sheer accident, Bill and Grace ended by not buying from him either, though they were sure they would call on him for any future insurance needs.

So they bought from the bank

It happened that Bill noticed a life-insurance display in the mutual-savings bank where he and Grace had a savings account. They were fortunate enough to live in one of the three states—Connecticut, Massachusetts and New York—in which mutual-savings banks sell life insurance. Their policies are among the most reasonably priced available, primarily because the banks do not engage salesmen, though they have competent advisors in their offices.

As we noted earlier, Bill and Grace had by this time decided that all they would buy for the present was a policy that would pay off the mortgage at his death.

So at the bank they bought a policy that would reduce the amount of protection each year as the amount of their mortgage declined. This is about the cheapest type of insurance available, and the bank's net price was better than that on any comparable policy they had seen.

Grace noted, along the way, that they would have gone to a savings bank in the first place had she not misplaced the list of life-insurance sources she had compiled. Bill scowled.

Some research and an inquiry to your state's insurance department can often turn up a variety of insurance sources in addition to the conventional life companies. Some sources are limited to residents of a particular state. For example, Wisconsin residents may buy up to $10,000 of life insurance at a quite reasonable cost from their state government. Life insurance often is obtainable through fraternal orders, professional associations and unions. Not to be overlooked, also, are credit unions, which offer their members life insurance, up to certain limits, on their savings accounts and loans. A form of life insurance is often available as part of a mutual fund accumulation plan to provide for completion of payments.

Policies generally should not be bought by mail. Aside from the fact that there is no personal counseling, the company may not be licensed to sell in your state, minimizing the benefit of your state's protection and maximizing the cost of litigation in the event of dispute.

There are several specific cautions that should be kept in mind when dealing with insurance agents:

• Be wary if the agent is persuasively promoting high-priced policies that have "tremendous savings that you could use in retirement" but that provide only a fraction of the protection you need now.

• Be wary if he urges that an existing policy be dropped in favor of his, unless he offers convincing arguments. This practice, known as "twisting," can be costly. It is illegal in some states.

• Steel yourself against pressure selling, or emotional spellbinding ("You owe it to your loved ones to invest in this policy for their sakes"), or the only slightly veiled immortality lure ("With investment in this protection now, your presence will be felt long after you have passed on"). You should suspect that the agent's real game is protecting his own income, for high-priced policies bring high commissions.

Reputable agents do not resort to tactics of this sort. They know that in the long run, honest consultation and good service pay off far more handsomely than does pressure selling. To them, insurance clients are long-term clients who will need more insurance as their families and incomes grow, and who have friends they can send to an agent they know and trust.

Many unsuitable life-insurance policies have been unwisely bought by people trapped by the spiels of unscrupulous salesmen bemoaning the fates of their loved ones.

CHAPTER III

Social Security Benefits for Survivors

A full analysis of the federal Social Security program is offered in another unit of this series, where it most appropriately belongs. But here we can usefully, if briefly, look into one aspect of the program that most people know little about: survivors' benefits that have the effect of life-insurance proceeds.

You may remember that Bill all but scoffed at Social Security benefits when he and his wife Grace embarked on their estate-planning project. He was quite startled to learn, however, how much Grace and their children would receive in benefits at his death. That, in fact, became the foundation of their estate plan.

We noted in that discussion that Bill's survivors' benefits would increase with each year that he worked, and that Congress could be expected to continue to liberalize Social Security payments. And in 1972 Congress voted several increases in benefits. As of September, 1972, the monthly benefit to Grace and her children would be $527.60 if Bill died.

Indeed, that blue and white Social Security identification card you carry in your wallet is one of your most valuable documents. It has a potential worth to you and your family of literally hundreds of thousands of dollars. Upon application, substantial cash benefits will be paid to your family at your death, to you and your family in the event of your total disability, or to you on retirement.

Use of Social Security benefits as a base for financial planning is a major selling point of the life-insurance industry. And it's a valid one.

The effect of the 1972 amendments was not only to make the survivors' benefits substantially higher than in the past but also to make them keep pace with inflation. After 1974, when the cost-of-living index rises 3% or more, benefits are to be proportionally increased.

A lot of people either ignore or downrate Social Security in their life-insurance planning. They shouldn't: Social Security survivors' benefits can be very important.

An insured worker's "Primary Insurance Benefit" is the key to all calculations of cash Social Security benefits. It is the amount he would receive each month, if he becomes totally disabled, or at 65, when he retires. His dependents or survivors would receive percentages of that amount. Calculation of the primary benefit is based on a worker's average monthly Social Security taxable income in the years worked after 1950.

For spouse, children and parents

Upon the death of an insured worker—the self-employed are also covered—Social Security benefits would be paid to his family, calculated as if his age were 65 at death. After application has been filed for benefits, the family receives a lump-sum death benefit of three times the monthly primary benefit, but no more than $255. Then, within the total family-benefit maximum, the surviving spouse would receive the primary benefit amount, and children would be entitled to a percentage. Within the limit, dependent parents of the insured also would be entitled to benefit payments.

No benefits would be available to a widow, if she is under 60, not disabled or caring for a child under age 18. At 60, she may apply for reduced "widow's benefits" but if she waits until she is 62 she is entitled to the full benefit.

A child would receive benefit payments until 18, or until 22 if he or she is a full-time student. A child who becomes totally disabled before age 18 is entitled to lifetime benefits.

Children are considered dependent on both their mother and father, and they may become eligible for benefits when either parent becomes entitled to retirement- or disability-benefits or dies.

Payments may also be made under certain conditions to a surviving divorced wife at 60 or 62 or to a disabled, surviving divorced wife who is 50 or older. To qualify for benefits, a divorced wife must have been married to the worker for 20 or more consecutive years and also meet certain support requirements. Benefits also can be paid to a dependent surviving divorced wife at any age if she is caring for a child of her late former husband if the child is under 18 or disabled.

Social Security benefits are not subject to federal income tax.

Calculating benefits due under the Social Security laws can be a complicated process but local offices of the agency can help mightily, and are usually cooperative in helping individuals who come in to them for assistance.

CHAPTER IV

The Four
Basic Types

Mary and Jack believed they had done their homework well in working up an estate plan. It seemed letter-perfect. It effectively utilized all their assets and resources, and showed precisely what their requirements were in additional life insurance.

This is how they figured out their problem:

Even with their existing insurance, including Jack's group coverage through his job, they needed additional protection, in the event of his premature death, to provide more investment capital. This would be needed to bring in supplemental income for Mary during the children's growing years. They also needed coverage that would pay off the mortgage.

A large part of the investment capital was intended eventually to finance the children's educations. So they needed to be sure that, together with the proceeds of the ultimate sale of the free-and-clear house, enough of the capital would be available, after the education bills were paid, to give Mary some measure of financial independence in her later years.

Also, if they could swing it, they wanted to buy some insurance on Mary's life to ease the economic pressure on the family should she die prematurely.

Their problem and the solution, they thought, were both simple.

Golly! No joke!

So, without being too selective, they saw several insurance agents. They were inundated with an overwhelming flood of proposals. They were offered:

- family plans
- family-income policies
- adjustable whole-life policies
- modified whole-life policies
- Presidential plans ("Golly!" Jack thought)
- endowments at age 95 (no joke!)
- retirement-income plans
- and more.

On hearing all this verbiage, Jack's eyes took on a dull glaze, and Mary gulped. Realizing now that they knew next to nothing about life insurance and the terminology of the industry, they did some reading.

PRESIDENTIAL PLAN

FAMILY INCOME PLAN

FAMILY PLAN

TERM PLAN

STRAIGHT LIFE

WHOLE LIFE POLICY

AGE 95 ENDOWMENT

ENDOWMENT

RETIREMENT INCOME

WHOLE LIFE

The life-insurance industry is a prolific coiner
of terminology. The names of various policies
obscure the fact that there are only four basic types.

They learned that they had to be more discriminating in the selection of an agent. Equally important, they learned that life insurance itself is not at all as complicated as they had been led to think. The industry only makes it look that way.

The life-insurance business is highly competitive for your dollar. Hundreds of merchandising-conscious, aggressive life-insurance companies try to entice you with literally thousands of different policies, many with high-sounding—or confusing—names. However, there are only four basic types of life insurance. The thousands of policies advertised are based on one or more of these four: term, whole (or straight) life, limited payment life and the endowment policy.

All four basic types of insurance naturally provide death protection. However, their premium rates vary widely because of variations in the "savings" feature.

The savings are the cash values that build up in certain kinds of policies. It is axiomatic that the faster that build-up is and the greater the ultimate cash value of a policy, the larger the premium is. And as the premium increases the amount of life insurance you receive for each dollar you pay goes down.

Nothing but protection

Term insurance nearly always has no build-up of cash value, so it usually has the lowest premium. All it offers is protection.

Whole life costs more than term, but it slowly builds its cash value over a lifetime of payments while providing protection, as its name implies.

Limited payment life provides lifetime protection but costs still more than whole life because it accumulates cash value at a faster rate. With this kind of policy premiums are paid within a stated period of time, or the payments end at a specified age, usually 65, while the protection continues.

The cash value of whole life and limited payment life never goes up to face value of the contract, the amount paid at death or at a specific time. Usually the maximum cash value of these policies is little more than 60%.

In a class by itself is endowment insurance. This is predominantly a savings vehicle, a fact that makes it one of the most expensive contracts. The cash value builds up to the face amount of the policy within a specified number of years, perhaps 20 or 30, or at a particular age of the insured person, such as 65.

The cash value is a form of savings that is counted among a man's assets, but it cannot be taken and used unless he gives up his policy. If he chooses not to surrender the policy, he may borrow against its cash value, at interest, from the insurance company. If he dies, the cash value is part of, not additional to, the face amount paid to his beneficiary. In effect, the beneficiary would get only the cash value

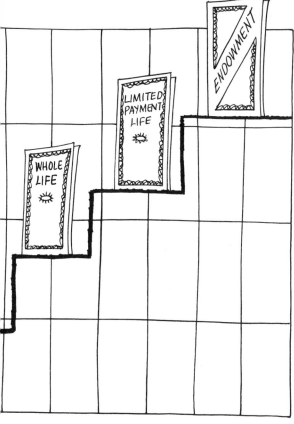

The price tags of the four basic types of policies
can vary considerably: you should comparison shop.

when it exceeded the insurance amount, as
might be the case with a costly retirement-
income contract.

Cash values have significance in terms of an insured person's gamble against death, or, perhaps
more accurately, in terms of a man's rationalization
about death. ("The other guy, but not me—not for a
long, long time.") If he lives, and he obviously feels
sure he will, he can personally enjoy the benefits of

the cash value of his policy or policies, possibly by making them a part of his retirement plan. But if he were certain that he would die before he could use them himself, then the additional cost of the savings feature obviously would be wasted.

Savings for the non-saving

By their nature, life-insurance savings are enforced, a feature that may make them attractive to people who find it difficult to put money aside consistently.

An analysis of a permanent policy shows why the cash value cannot be taken without surrendering the policy. It also shows how it is possible to have level premium payments. In a level premium policy, the same amount of money is paid in each year of the premium-payment period, whether that be 10 or 20 years, or to a specified age.

In the early years of the policy, when the insured person is young and statistically less likely to die, and when the policy's cash value is small, he is paying more than enough to buy the proportionately large amount of insurance needed to make up the face amount. Those overpayments become part of the cash value or reserve. In the later years of the policy, when the insured person's statistical chance of dying is greater and the cost of insurance is correspondingly higher, he can still pay the same premium as he did in the earlier years because now less insurance is needed to make up the difference between the cash value, which has grown, and the face amount, which has not.

To illustrate the level premium concept, under which the insurance factor steadily reduces over the years while the "savings"—or cash-value—factor increases, let's examine a $10,000 whole-life policy. It was bought by a 30-year-old man who will pay a premium of $227 a year.

End of Policy Year	Cash or Loan Value	Insurance Needed To Make Up $10,000 Face Amount
1	$ 0	$10,000
2	120	9,880
3	290	9,710
4	450	9,550
5	620	9,380
6	790	9,210
7	960	9,040
8	1,140	8,860
9	1,320	8,680
10	1,500	8,500
11	1,660	8,340
12	1,820	8,180
13	1,980	8,020
14	2,150	7,850
15	2,320	7,680
16	2,490	7,510
17	2,660	7,340
18	2,830	7,170
19	3,000	7,000
20	3,180	6,820
21	3,350	6,650
22	3,530	6,470
23	3,700	6,300
24	3,880	6,120
25	4,050	5,950
30	4,930	5,070

A paid-up policy may have a cash value of only 60% of the face amount of protection, but that reserve is invested by the insurance company, together with other policy reserves, to yield enough—and sometimes more than enough—to pay for the insurance needed to make up the difference of 40%.

Permanent insurance—whole-life or limited-payment life—has opponents. They argue that it is merely a combination of an ever-increasing savings account with a decreasing face-amount of term insurance, which as its name suggests, goes down in insurance value each year.

They say that the savings feature of permanent insurance is a poor savings account, so an insured person would be better off buying his own decreasing term insurance and investing the savings portion more profitably through other savings or investment channels. We will discuss more fully this concept—"buy-term-and-invest-the-difference"—later.

Conservative dissenters say that permanent insurance ought to have a limited role in a family's life-insurance program. In the early years, when the children are young and insurance needs are greatest, a man can stretch his insurance dollars by building a tower of inexpensive term-insurance protection on a foundation of relatively expensive permanent insurance.

In later years, when his income may be reduced, and when insurance needs are also generally reduced, the man can retain all or part of his permanent insurance because it has now become relatively inexpensive, thanks to the level-premium feature, whereas term insurance for a man his age would have become much more expensive than it was when he was young. If he has more permanent policies than he seems to need, he can surrender the surplus for the cash value, which becomes supplemental income.

On expiration, nothing

Now let's take a closer look at the four basic types of insurance. And, while we're at it, let's see, in general terms, why Mary and Jack selected what they did to make up their life-insurance program.

• Term life insurance: It can be likened to automobile or fire insurance in that it provides protection for a specified period of time, and returns nothing to the buyer when it expires. A term policy may pay dividends, if it is a higher-premium participating contract, but it has no cash-value build-up. If a so-called term policy shows cash-value build-up, it may be a level-premium term policy of long duration. This may have some cash value in the early years, at least in theory. This comes about because a premium rate that is higher than necessary is levied in the early years to make up for the greater risk in the later years. Otherwise it would be impossible to offer a level premium for a long period.

Term insurance is usually written for one year, or for 5 or 10 years. Some companies offer it for longer periods or up to a particular age, sometimes as advanced as 65. The vast majority of group plans, like those provided as an employment fringe benefit, are straight term insurance; some of these may protect employees beyond age 65.

You can buy term as a separate policy or in combination with permanent life insurance. The premium rates are low at early ages but climb steeply for older buyers. Putting aside the cash values and other promoted features of permanent policies, term insurance always requires a smaller cash outlay for death protection than any other form of individual insurance available at the time that you buy it.

You will readily see this in a table in the appendix which presents typical yearly costs of $1,000 of life insurance for men at different ages. (The figures can and do vary from company to company. Those shown in our table are provided by the Institute of Life Insurance.) The table shows the cost of $1,000 of coverage provided by a nonparticipating policy as well as by a participating policy, which pays dividends, the size of which depends on the actuarial experience of the company issuing the policy. There is no set formula.

The cost of each $1,000 of protection is generally reduced when large policies, $10,000 or more, are bought. What you get, in effect, is a quantity discount. And, because women generally live longer than men, they usually pay less for life insurance. Women's premium rates generally are those of men three years younger.

As you grow older, year by year, term-insurance rates increase, because increasing age brings a statistically greater risk of death. The premium rates for term policies of longer than one-year duration remain the same each year that the policy is in force, and are an approximate average of the rates that would have been charged if the policies had been rated year by year.

There are two term-policy provisions you should consider asking for, though they add slightly to the cost: 1) the right to renew; 2) the right to convert to permanent insurance. Both provisions should stipulate that they do not require a medical examination or other proof of insurability.

With these provisions one can know he will be able to maintain his insurance program, usually to age 65, even if his health deteriorates in the meantime to the extent of making him otherwise uninsurable.

Some states make convertibility mandatory.

A highly flexible and useful form of term insurance is decreasing-face amount, which can be bought separately or as part of a permanent policy. The maximum coverage it offers at the beginning of its long protection period, up to 25 years or more, or to a specified age, gradually reduces to zero by the end of the period. The annual cost remains constant.

Some companies charge somewhat more than is necessary, but they charge nothing at all in the last several years of a long decreasing-face term policy. This is to discourage policyholders from canceling in later years, when the amount of protection is relatively small. At that time, if they still were paying premiums, the payments would appear to be inordinately large for the protection they provided. In cases of this sort the company, in effect, collects the premiums for those later years in advance, thus locking the policyholders in. If you think about it, you will probably agree that the practice is not entirely unfair.

Decreasing term is ideal for families wishing to have the steadily decreasing unpaid balance on a home mortgage or other major loan paid off at death, or to leave the family with supplemental funds for the children's growing years, which steadily reduce in number.

• Whole life: This is the most widely sold of the permanent policies, with cash-value accumulation and level-premium payments. It is known by many other names, among them "straight" and "ordinary" life. However, any policy of $1,000 or more on an individual, with premiums payable annually, semi-annually, quarterly or monthly, is technically ordinary life.

Whole life provides lifetime protection in exchange for lifetime payment of premiums. The premium rate is understandably greater than that of term insurance, but it is the lowest of all types of permanent insurance, and therefore provides the most in permanent protection for the dollar.

Whole life is the bread-and-butter contract of most insurance companies. For this reason they often attempt to dress it up with impressive-sounding names. The zaniest of these is "endowment at 95," which means that the insured himself would receive the face amount, if he were alive at age 95. This is true of any whole-life policy, since it would mature, i.e., pay off the face amount, when the insured dies—actuarially or actually. For insurance purposes, actuarial death is up around age 95. That's a couple of dozen years beyond reality.

Whatever they may call it, many companies offer whole life at slightly reduced rates in larger policies, usually $10,000 or more in face amount. In doing this they are passing on savings in administrative costs realized by issuing and servicing one large policy rather than several small ones.

• Limited payment: This differs from whole life in premium-payment procedure only. The rates are higher, and the payments are made over a specified period, usually 20 or 30 years or to a particular age, such as 65. The result is that the build-up of cash value is faster. Completing all premium payments in a relatively few years may sound like a good idea, but we must keep in mind that this type of policy provides less protection for each premium dollar. It would not well serve a family that has limited funds for insurance and needs the most protection it can get with those funds.

On the other hand, it may appeal particularly to professional athletes, entertainers and other persons whose incomes may be large over a relatively small number of years, and then drop drastically.

• Endowment: Primarily a savings policy, and an expensive one. It is written for a specified period of

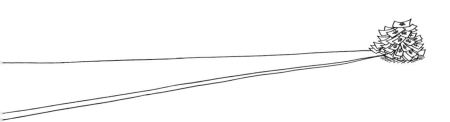

Endowment policies—very expensive—don't pay off
for many, many years, which explains why they are believed
to appeal largely to people with an "immortality syndrome."

time, perhaps 20 or 30 years, or to a particular age, the most common again being 65. If the insured person dies in that period, the beneficiary would receive the face amount. If he lives to its end, he gets it himself. This idea appeals to many people, particularly those caught up in the immortality syndrome. But the same disadvantages of the limited payment plan are present—in spades—because endowments are so much more costly. Furthermore, the greater the savings and investment features of a policy, the more skeptical you must be about the quality of the savings and investment vehicle. Can you do better by putting the money to work elsewhere? Chances are you can.

No savings, only the face amount

If a person dies in the 19th year of a 20-year limited-payment policy or, worse yet, of a 20-year endowment, the beneficiary would get only the face amount.

The insured person's large "savings" would be helping to make up that face amount, about 95% of it in the case of the endowment and more than half in the limited payment policy. The price of either of these expensive policies would have bought considerably greater protection in whole-life or term insurance. Or less costly insurance in the same amount might have been bought, and the cost difference saved or invested for the benefit of the insured or his survivors.

Even more expensive than the endowment is the retirement-income policy, a savings contract that ceases to be an insurance policy when the cash value exceeds the face amount. At death, the face amount or cash value, whichever is greater, is payable to the beneficiary. The retirement policy differs from the endowment in that, at maturity, usually at age 65, it pays a monthly income, rather than a lump sum.

Getting back to Mary and Jack, to whom we introduced you at the beginning of this chapter, they more carefully selected a reputable insurance agent, and then put to work their newly acquired insurance knowledge in dealing with him.

Following their estate plan, they supplemented Jack's $35,000 of group-life insurance with a $20,000 whole-life policy. At 35, that cost him about $440 a year. He also added a $500 monthly family-income provision that spanned a 20-year period. If Jack died within the 20-year period, his family would receive $500 a month for the balance of the period.

Over 20 years, down to zero

Their plan was that, at Jack's death, Mary would get the commuted, or cash, value of the family-income provision, along with the face value of the basic whole-life policy. The family-income provision, was, in effect, a decreasing-term policy.

At $500 monthly, at inception it had a commuted value of some $79,000, with interest figured at 4% compounded quarterly. Though this would steadily reduce over the 20 years to zero, at the start of the 20-year period, the family had $134,000 in protection against Jack's untimely death ($35,000 in group, $20,-000 in whole life, $79,000 in term). At the end of the period, there would be $55,000 in protection. Even that wouldn't remain static, because Jack's group insurance would increase over the years, as his salary grew.

Jack and Mary decided they didn't need a separate mortgage-redemption policy. Even after paying off the mortgage, there would be enough insurance money left to provide supplemental income for Mary and the kids. By the time the 20 years were up, the children would have been grown and the mortgage paid off. The insurance protection, even though much reduced by then, plus other assets and resources, would be enough to cover Mary's needs at Jack's death.

Able to protect against his untimely death at less cost than had been expected, the couple saw the way clear to buy a $30,000 decreasing-term policy on Mary's life. That would make things easier for Jack and the children, if she died prematurely.

Mary and Jack were so pleased with themselves for having completed this job, with all its unpleasant overtones (or is it undertones?), that they decided to celebrate with a fancy dinner—out. There may be greater reasons to celebrate, but who said anyone needed a reason anyhow?

CHAPTER V

Putting Life Insurance into Packages

Like ingredients for a fancy cake, the four basic forms of life insurance can be blended into a variety of concoctions, some rather indigestible, but many quite palatable, and with lots of eye appeal, too.

But remember that the only right "concoction" for you in life insurance is the policy that best meets your needs within your ability to pay for it. Pricing is competitive, so you ought to shop. Remember also that any capable insurer generally can make up the combinations, or "packages," that other insurance companies are offering.

Perhaps the most popular combination contract is the "family-income policy." The policy is a combina-

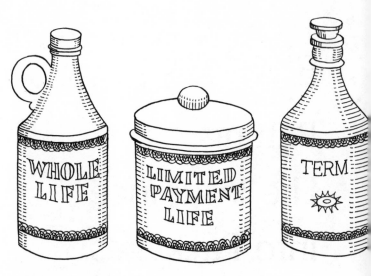

Getting the right blend of life-insurance policies for your particular situation cal

tion of decreasing-term insurance and basic permanent coverage, usually whole life. Once the decreasing-term portion has expired, the cost is reduced to that of the basic permanent policy.

A family-income policy provides supplemental income to a family in the years when the children are growing up and living costs are high. The most typical period is 20 years, reckoned from the date of the purchase of the policy.

r a lot of thought. You're mixing ingredients for a very important cake.

If the insured person dies within that period, his beneficiary receives $10 a month in "family income" for each $1,000 of the basic policy's face amount for the balance of the 20 years. That would be 1% a month of the policy's face amount. (Some companies offer 1½ or 2%—or even as much as 4%—at a higher cost.) In addition, the beneficiary also receives the policy's face amount, in cash or additional income, at the insured person's death or at the end of the family-income period, depending on the contract. Most companies provide this money at the time of death, and that is what you should look for.

You may decide to have your beneficiary get the commuted value—immediate cash—of the family-income plan at your death. If you want the decision to be left to the beneficiary, you have to add that option to the policy if it isn't already there.

The commuted value would be that portion of the decreasing-term insurance that remained. To illustrate: Take a $10,000 whole-life policy carrying a 20-year family-income rider providing $100, or 1% of the face amount of the basic policy, in monthly payments during the family-income period. There is available some $15,800 in cash in the first year.

If the insured person dies immediately after buying the policy, his beneficiary receives $25,800, including the $15,800 commuted value of the family income and the $10,000 of basic coverage. In the 10th year, the commuted value drops to less than $10,000, reducing the total immediate cash payment to less than $20,000.

The "family-maintenance policy" is a variation on the family-income package. The difference is that the family-income period begins with the insured's death, not with the purchase date. Thus, if 20 years of payments are stipulated, the 20-year income period begins after the insured dies, provided that he dies within 20 years after he had bought the policy.

If a man buys this kind of policy in 1972 and dies in 1982, his family would receive monthly income until 2002. If he had bought a family-income policy instead, the monthly payments would have stopped in 1992, or 20 years after purchase.

The family-maintenance policy is more expensive, and some authorities seriously question whether its obvious advantage is valuable in most family situations.

Another plan that should not be confused with either the family-income or family-maintenance plans is the "family policy." This one insures the whole family, and is usually issued in units of $5,000. The father would have whole-life insurance protection in that amount, the wife would be covered by $1,000 or $1,250 of term insurance and each of the children would have $1,000 of term protection. Large families interested in insuring children find this policy especially economical, for each child is automatically covered 15 days after birth at no added cost.

You must realize that these and any other special features of a policy cost money, and the extras can cut deeply enough into a family's insurance allotment to leave the father underinsured.

Still another contract that combines whole life and term is the "extra-protection policy." Not widely offered, it provides "extra protection" which usually continues to age 60 or 65. This may be $1,000, $2,000 or sometimes $3,000 of term insurance added for each $1,000 of basic whole-life protection.

This extra coverage provides less protection for the extra-premium dollar than does the family-income plan, but it can be carried for a longer period. For example, you may add $10,000 to $30,000 of extra term protection to a $10,000 permanent policy, keeping the extra coverage to age 60 or 65, depending on the insurance company issuing it. It's not widely available.

A "modified life policy" is designed for those who cannot afford all the family protection they now need but expect their incomes to improve significantly within a few years. They may be, for example, young physicians or other professionals. The policy provides low-cost term insurance for perhaps three to five years, after which it automatically converts to a whole-life policy, with the premium rate rising accordingly.

If you are in excellent health, are in the safest of occupations and can buy at least $10,000 of insurance (sometimes the minimum is as much as $25,000), then you would be attracted to the "preferred risk policy."

This contract, usually standard whole-life protection, is offered at appreciably reduced rates to those who can qualify. The saving may be as much as 10% of the standard rates. These policies, too, can generally be obtained by an astute shopper, though agents may not be pushing them enthusiastically.

A security or a life insurance policy?

Two other packages are something of a departure from those we have been discussing: "split-life" and "variable-life" plans. You should be aware of them though they may never be available to you.

At this writing, the first is not legal in New York and is under close scrutiny in several other states. The second, variable life, is being studied by the federal Securities and Exchange Commission to determine whether it is a security—and therefore subject to the agency's regulation—or a life-insurance policy—and therefore to be watchdogged by the states.

Under the split-life concept, two separate policies are sold as a package. One is an annual-premium, deferred annuity. The other is a very low-cost term policy that is renewable each year at stepped-up but still comparatively low rates to an advanced age (in one case, 100).

The attractively priced term insurance cannot be bought unless the annuity is bought with it, and that tie-in sale appears to be the primary criticism of state insurance regulators who are opposed to the plan.

Contracting for income

An annuity is a contract that provides an income for a specified period, such as a number of years, or for life, after all premiums have been paid. The beneficiary, at the death of the annuitant during the premium-payment years, would receive a return of premium payments or the cash value, whichever is greater.

Annuities are expensive; the question is, aren't there better investment vehicles?

Under the split-life plan, the purchaser of an annuity may buy term insurance in an amount up to 100 times the annuity's annual premium. Thus, if the annuity premium is $1,000 a year, term life up to $100,-000 may be bought along with it. And, most interestingly, the life insurance may be on the lives of any number of persons other than the annuitant, provided that they are insurable and there is an insurable connection between insured and beneficiary.

There are a number of suggested applications of the plan. Two are in employment situations and in charitable giving.

A company may buy a $10,000-a-year-premium annuity for the benefit of its head, and a substantial amount of term life insurance— up to $1,000,000—on the lives of several key employees.

Or a man may make his alma mater or favorite charity the beneficiary of the annuity, and take the cheap insurance on his own life. Thus he gets life insurance at the lowest possible cost, while making systematic, tax-deductible contributions.

Theme for lawyer, agent and consultant

There are many variations on these themes. However, if such a plan is offered in your area, and you think it might be right for you, don't make a move without the advice of a reputable insurance agent, your lawyer and a tax consultant. The apparent tax advantages and certain other aspects of the plan still are subject to challenge at this juncture.

Under a variable life insurance contract, the death benefit and other benefits would vary, above a minimum stated amount, to reflect the gains (or losses) of a separate securities-investment account maintained by the life-insurance company. The premiums would not vary. This is designed as protection against inflation, on the theory that the prices of securities rise in inflationary times. Thus, as securities prices rose, so would death benefits paid out of invested funds.

The life-insurance industry is fighting federal regulation on this, fearful that dual regulation (federal and state) would be costly and cumbersome. This has kept the contract off the marketplace and will continue to do so for some time, if not indefinitely.

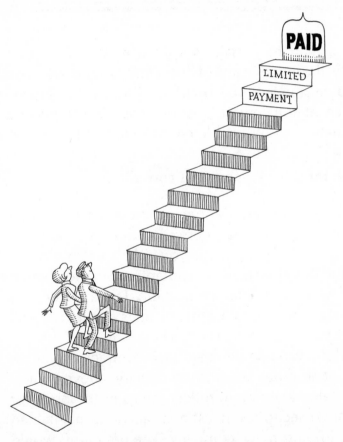

Different kinds of life insurance may have different appeals for different people. Some may prefer the limited-premium type, which are paid up in full after a specified number of payments.

CHAPTER VI

What Does
It Really
Cost?

With so much industry emphasis on the savings features of permanent-life insurance and promotion of its so-called investment aspects, it's not to be wondered that so much attention—and controversy—has centered on the question of the true cost of life insurance's primary function: death protection.

As we shall see, determining how much life insurance really costs is no easy task. Ideally a simple formula could be applied to comparable policies and spotlight the contract with the lowest net cost and greatest advantage to you as a buyer. Progress has been made toward creating such a simple formula but it still doesn't exist.

Nevertheless, it is worth your effort to calculate comparative net cost despite the many complications and imponderables. If nothing else, the exercise will give you a better understanding of the life-insurance apparatus, and this will help you to develop the program of economic protection prescribed by your family-estate plan.

We're not talking about the annual net outlay, which is simple enough to figure. That's the premium paid, minus dividends, if any. The topic here is the true long-term cost, the actual net cost, on surrender.

Through their agents, insurance companies have for years presented prospective buyers with net-cost illustrations that could be misleading. Generally referred to as the "traditional method" of calculating net cost, the illustration usually is a 20-year projection. They work it out this way: anticipated dividends, if any, are deducted from the total amount of the premium payments that are called for. So are also the 20-year cash or surrender values (as stipulated in

The ways of figuring the costs of life insurance
can seem terrifyingly complex. Do your
homework to learn what questions to ask.

the policy) plus any termination dividend that may be included.

What's left is considered the 20-year net cost. Dividing that figure by 20 would give the annual net cost of the policy. That, in turn, could be divided by the number of thousands of dollars of the policy's face amount, which would give the annual net cost per $1,000 of protection.

One way to figure the net

Here's an arithmetical example of the traditional method, purportedly showing the 20-year average payments and net costs for a $10,000 whole-life policy issued to a 35-year-old man. The annual premium is $240, and the annual dividend is projected at $18 at the end of the first year, increasing by $6 each year thereafter. It would reach $132 in the 20th year. There would be no cash value in the first year, but it would accumulate thereafter by $190 each year to $3,610 at the end of the 20th year.

Total premiums	$ 4,800
Less total dividends	1,500
Net cost	3,300
Less 20-year cash value	3,610
Actual 20-year insurance cost	−310
Cost per year	−15.50
Annual cost per $1,000 of Insurance	−1.55

Thus it would appear that the buyer of this policy would actually realize a profit if he cashed in his policy at the end of 20 years. He would get $3,610 upon surrender of his policy, $310 more than his total premium payments, minus dividends. So the actual insurance protection would be free. . . .

That would look like a great deal to an unthinking consumer.

Quite frequently, calculation of net insurance cost by the traditional method results in a negative factor or an apparent profit to the buyer. This makes it a great sales tool. Unfortunately, the underlying logic and mathematics of the procedure are faulty.

It does show what the buyer's net outlay would be: 1) if the company's current dividend scale remained unchanged (actually it could go up or down) and 2) if the policyholder were to surrender his policy for its cash value at the end of the projected period (20 years in our illustration). But it ignores the interest potential because it fails to consider the time when a dollar is paid by the policyholder, or when a dollar is paid to him.

Conscious of criticism on this ground, three major industry associations—the American Life Convention, the Institute of Life Insurance and the Life Insurance Association of America—appointed a Joint Special Committee on Life Insurance Costs. This committee studied about a dozen methods, but concluded, in a

1970 report, that the "interest-adjusted method" was the "most suitable" because it does take time of payment into account, and it is relatively easy to understand. While its similarities to the traditional method should simplify its adoption, most companies had not made the transition by the end of 1972.

The committee recommended that a 4% annual interest rate be used, because it is near what you might earn, after taxes, on a long-term savings account.

Here is an example of the interest-adjusted method that was included in the committee's report. It has been applied to the same $10,000 policy used in our illustration of the traditional method, which also came from the committee's report.

Total of 20 annual premiums, each
  accumulated at 4% $7,433.00
Less 20 yearly dividends, each
  accumulated at 4% .... −2,003.00
Net premiums over 20 years 5,430.00
Less 20-year cash value in policy ...... −3,160.00
20-year insurance cost 1,820.00

Earnings of $1 a year at
  4% interest 30.97
Interest-adjusted annual cost
  ($1,820 divided by $30.97) 58.77
Annual cost per $1,000 of insurance
  ($58.77 divided by 10) 5.88

Putting it another way: if you took that interest-adjusted annual cost of $58.77 and deposited it each year in a savings account that paid you an after-tax net of 4% interest, compounded annually, you would have $1,820 at the end of 20 years. An annual deposit of $240 (equal to the annual premium) in the same type of savings account would grow to $7,433 in 20 years.

However, if you bought the policy, and paid $240 annually for 20 years, and then cashed it in, you would get only $5,613 (the $3,610 in cash value and the $2,003 in dividends, if you had left them to accumulate at interest). The $1,820 difference ($7,433 minus $5,613) would be your payment for 20 years of insurance protection.

Do you have the wisdom? The will?

The interest-adjusted method is considerably more realistic than the traditional method, but even this is really no more than a comparative-cost guide. A number of factors are not taken into account. For example, you may have the wisdom and skill to generate considerably greater investment income than the 4% per year on which the interest-adjusted method is predicated. That alone would cause your net insurance cost to soar, because the difference between what you would receive in surrender cash-value and dividends over 20 years and the amount you would have generated by putting your premium dollars to work in other investments might be far greater than that shown in our illustration.

However attractive a policy's net cost is, you can't

take advantage of it without surrendering your protection. Therefore the keystone of any net-cost formula is the contract's cash value. Thus, net cost can
be meaningful to you only if you know that you're
not going to die, and that you no longer will need
the insurance protection beyond a certain age. If you
die prematurely, the policy's cash value, in effect, dies
with you, for it is part of, not additional to, the face
amount that your beneficiary would receive. In that
case, the cash-value amount must be added to your
net insurance cost.

This is a fact that many people do not understand, and many a beneficiary is shocked to
discover that he or she is receiving only the
face value of the contract, not the face plus the
cash value.

You were warned that this business of net cost
could get complicated. In some respects, it could also
be somewhat academic, particularly to the family
man who is not in an economic position to choose
between investments and essential life-insurance protection. Besides, any purchase, whether it be life insurance, an auto or a can opener, could spark discussion of what the purchase price might have earned
if invested or put into a bank. The conclusion would
probably be that the actual cost of the product or

Some people think that with a
life-insurance policy that has cash-value build-up,
the beneficiary gets the face amount plus
the cash value. Definitely not so:
the beneficiary gets only the face amount.

service was the price paid plus the earnings "lost" by
that money if used otherwise.

Like any other product or service, life insurance
costs money, no matter how you figure it. If the long-
term net cost is relatively low, then there's a strong
probability that the policy has a high premium rate
per $1,000 of coverage and a relatively rapid and large
cash-value build-up. Thus, the policy owner's apparent long-term net cost is low, primarily because

he is providing the insurance company with investment capital (the cash value), and the income he
loses on that capital is part of his total cost.

Opponents of permanent insurance recom-
mend that an insurance buyer strive for his
own low-net-cost plan of investment and insurance. Their recommendation centers on
purchase of the cheapest form of insurance—
pure term—and investment of the extra money
that would have been spent on more expensive
policies. This is the concept known as "buy-
term-and-invest-the-difference."

Applied in the right circumstances, this concept
could put an insured person way ahead of the game.
Under the classic version of the plan, you buy term
insurance, including a good deal of decreasing-face
amount term, all of which provides initial protection
equal to your total life-insurance needs.

Then you determine the difference in cost between
that protection and the more conventional coverage,
including a substantial foundation of higher-premium
permanent insurance. In each premium-payment
period, you invest that difference. Thus you build up
your own "cash values." Your investment fund, according to the advocates, ultimately more than off-

One life-insurance suggestion: buy term insurance rather than
more costly permanent policies. Put what you save on
the premiums into investments with a better yield than life insurance.

sets the decline in insurance protection afforded by
the decreasing-term policies.

As you advance in age (perhaps to your mid 40s),
you convert a sufficient amount of the term insurance
to permanent policies, so as to stabilize your annual
outlay for the basic protection you would need for
the rest of your life. This basic protection might be to
cover death expenses, a lifetime income for your
spouse and an emergency fund.

What are the right circumstances in which it is wise
to buy term and invest the difference?

1) The buyer must be highly disciplined, capable of systematically investing the "difference" as if he were meeting regular bills. Too often a person starts the program, and then finds other uses for the money that should have been invested.

2) He or she must be capable of selecting the right savings or investment vehicle, or of selecting the right advisers.

3) His or her economic position and life-insurance program must be such that they warrant consideration of such a program. In other words, a man who can just barely afford term insurance to meet at least part of his insurance needs doesn't have to consider the "difference."

Basically, the task of many insurance buyers is to achieve the fine balance between being underinsured and being "insurance poor," which is to say, being broke because so much income is paid out for insurance. The basic objective may simply be to match the amount of insurance a family's budget will allow with the amount of insurance a survey indicates is needed.

To go as far as possible toward filling as much of the life insurance requirement as their budgets will

For those who can't save, life insurance with cash-value build-up is enforced savings, keeping them from frittering away money that might be needed for emergencies.

allow, many families rely heavily on various forms of term insurance. A typical family may buy the least expensive permanent insurance (whole life) to provide lifetime protection against the continuing economic risks of death. Its shorter-term needs—for family income, for mortgage protection, for education and for other special funds—could be met with term, much of which can be bought at the lowest cost in combination with the permanent insurance. And, because certain of these needs generally reduce with the passing years and possibly with the growth of the family's other assets, they can be satisfied with a minimal cash outlay by the purchase of decreasing-face amount of term.

Insurance for special situations

Are high-cash-value permanent policies good for special situations? Yes. For example, if you are in a relatively high income-tax bracket, you might be attracted to the "minimum-deposit" scheme.

Under this concept, you would buy a special rapid cash-value build-up policy unit, and borrow against the cash value as it builds. You use the loans to help pay the premiums. This would be a participating policy, and you would use your dividends, under the so-called "fifth dividend option," to buy sufficient term insurance each year to offset your policy loan so as not to reduce the face amount of protection.

Various forms of term insurance can make up essential
parts in overall family planning for specific
purposes at specific times, while more costly whole-
life insurance is regarded as a long-term commitment.

The cash outlay for the amount of protection provided would be relatively small, according to proponents of the plan.

For example, suppose a 30-year-old man bought a $50,000 whole-life policy that cost $1,200 a year. There are quick cash-build-up policies that show a cash value in the first policy year, but let's suppose this is a more conventional policy that doesn't begin building cash values until the second year. In that year, and in each year thereafter, $950 is added to cash value.

And the loans pay the premiums

The insured man may borrow up to that amount each year, less the interest due on the mounting loan, and use the loan proceeds to help pay his premium. Thus, in the second policy year, he may borrow $900, and pay only $300 in cash to make up the total premium of $1,200. In the third year, he may have to reduce his loan to $850, laying out $350 in new cash to make up the premium difference. He conceivably could do this indefinitely, until he no longer needed the insurance, at which time he could surrender the policy and cancel the loans with the cash value that otherwise would have been his on surrender.

In the meantime, he would be using his dividends each year to buy one-year term insurance equal to his outstanding policy loans, plus interest. In that way, his face amount of insurance would not be reduced by the loans at his death. Depending on his particular insurance company's dividend projection, his dividend after the first year would be $90, and would increase each year by $30, so that after the second it would be $120, the third $150, and so on. The dividend amounts should be more than enough to pay for the ever-increasing one-year term policies, and the surplus dividend money could be used to offset the mounting policy-loan interest bill. That would allow him to borrow that much more of the cash-value increments.

The outlay may be further reduced after several years, when the insured person may become qualified for a tax advantage. He would then be allowed to reduce his taxable income each year by the amount of interest paid (with additional loans) on his policy loan—as may be done on any other loan.

Several years ago, you would have had that tax advantage from the beginning of the plan. Now, however, the Internal Revenue Service imposes restrictions, the principal one being that the taxpayer must have owned the policy at least 3 years before he can claim tax relief on the interest paid for a policy loan. The IRS made this ruling because it decided that the minimum-deposit plan was essentially an artificial loan scheme designed primarily to reduce the income-tax bill of an individual in a high tax bracket—and to sell him high-priced insurance.

CHAPTER VII

Group, Credit and Substandard-Risk Insurance

Group life is usually term insurance; that is, the premium collected for the entire group buys protection only from year to year. There is no permanent protection. Among the advantages to all participants: there is usually no medical examination required; the employer often pays part, and sometimes all, of the premium. The employee's payment, if any, is deducted from his paycheck, with his consent.

An employee loses his group insurance when he leaves his job. However, if he acts within a month, he can buy an individual policy from the insurance company in the same amount of protection as his group coverage. The premium rate would be that of his age. No medical examination is required, so he may even be uninsurable at the time.

Group-life insurance used to end when an employee retired. Now it often is continued by his employer, but usually in a reduced amount. In some cases, the reduction is immediate, and to a nominal $1,000 or $2,000. In others, the reduction is made in

The cheapest form of life insurance is group. The issuing company has to issue only one policy to cover a number of people, so everybody saves.

steps over a five-year period to about half of the benefit in force prior to his retirement.

A new development: in recent years various plans of group permanent-life insurance have been formulated. These cost more, but the employee leaving his job retains some part of his group protection as fully paid permanent insurance. In addition, he has the right to buy an individual policy, without evidence of insurability, equal to the balance of his group protection.

An important part of many family life insurance programs is the protection obtained through group life plans maintained by employers and other organizations. As you may recall, this was included in the estate plans developed by Bill and Grace and by Jack and Mary. It may be important in your situation, too.

Group insurance may be available to you through your employer, through a professional or trade association, a labor union, fraternal organization or other social or business group. Introduced in 1911, group-life insurance, as its name implies, provides the means for insuring a group of people under one policy which is called a master contract. Each participant in a group receives a certificate of insurance stating the amount of his insurance and a summary of his rights and benefits.

Essentially, group insurance is comparatively inexpensive because the insurance company has only nominal administrative costs. A large number of persons are protected under the master policy, which is issued by the insurance company in a single sale and is paid for in large sums by the employer or sponsoring organization. Most of the bookkeeping is done by the employer or sponsor. The cost advantage is especially great for older people in the group, for the price per $1,000 of coverage is an average for the group, predicated on the median age of the participants—i.e., half of the people are under that age and half are over.

There is a tax limitation on group-life insurance that other types of life insurance can escape. Your employer may be willing to help you escape it here. As noted earlier, life insurance proceeds go directly to the beneficiary and are not subject to income taxes. However, they are counted as part of the insured person's estate for estate-tax purposes.

This particular tax bite on the estate can be avoided by passing ownership of the policy to the beneficiary—who must then pay the premiums.

The Internal Revenue Service recognizes this procedure as valid. It also agrees that even an unemployed wife can pay the premiums, among other bills, with that part of her husband's income that she can claim as her own.

A special note: it must be proved to the IRS's satisfaction that the shift in policy ownership, if it took place within three years of death, was not made in the knowledge that that event was about to occur.

The problem with group-life insurance in this connection stems from the fact that the premiums are paid by payroll deduction. You could assign ownership of your group-life insurance to, say, your wife, but you must be able to rid yourself of all incidents of its ownership, such as the right to change the beneficiary—and the payment of premiums.

Your boss would therefore have to agree not to deduct your insurance payments from your paycheck, and to allow your wife periodically to write a personal check in payment of the premiums. If he agrees to do this, you could have reasonable assurance that this legal tax benefit would not be subject to challenge.

The proceeds of credit-life insurance are used to pay off a personal loan if the borrower dies before completing the payments. Some credit-life contracts also include a disability provision, and pay off the debt if the insured person becomes permanently and totally disabled.

Creditors often insist on this coverage, because it means they get their money even if the debtor dies, or, where it applies, becomes permanently and totally disabled.

Life-insurance proceeds earmarked for named beneficiaries, and not an estate, cannot be touched. And in general, a person's survivors, however much they may be badgered, have no responsibility to pay the decedent's debts. But since many people leave some sort of estate that could be subject to a creditor's claims, credit life can be beneficial to their heirs.

Credit life insurance is taken out to insure
a borrower. If he is disabled or dies, the proceeds
are used to pay off the loan.

Introduced in 1917, when installment buying became more prevalent in this country, credit life was provided under master contracts issued to banks and other types of lending agencies, and to retail stores that sell goods and services on installment plans.

While credit-life insurance rates generally are fair, the buyer should demand to be shown in the sales or loan contract just what the insurance coverage is— and the cost. There have been instances of overcharges. If the borrower is suspicious, even though he cannot compare insurance costs, he should ask for advice from his state's insurance department.

Some people cannot obtain standard life insurance at standard rates because of health defects, or because their occupations are considered to be hazardous. However, many of them can buy insurance by paying higher premiums. The amount of the surcharge varies with the reason for rejection as a normal insurance risk.

In recent years, an encouraging trend in this area of life insurance has become apparent: insurance companies are becoming relatively more liberal in their dealings with substandard risks.

If you want more life insurance, but think you might be rated as a substandard risk because of some ailment or physical impairment, you should first check with your own physician. If the condition is temporary or can be corrected, it would be wiser for you to wait, if possible, until you are reasonably sure that you can qualify as a standard risk. The primary reason for this is that if a substandard-risk policy is bought and the reason for the substandard rating is afterwards eliminated, it is often difficult and time-consuming to have the policy converted to a standard one.

What one company knows about you, all know

However, if your insurance need is pressing and too long a period of time might elapse before the ailment or impairment is eliminated, you may be unable to wait.

You should bear in mind, incidentally, that if a life-insurance medical examination causes an application for coverage to be rejected, the findings of that examination are available to all other life-insurance companies. This may make it difficult to buy a policy at some future time, even though the deficiency may have been corrected by then.

Anyone who is uninsurable or, at the very least, a substandard risk, should perhaps consider all avenues to obtain life insurance without a medical examination or other proof of individual insurability. He may be able to obtain group insurance through his employment or through a fraternal order or other organization. He could take group credit life on any indebtedness he has. In addition, if he has access to a

credit union, he might consider joining it and putting savings into a share account which is, in reality, a savings account. As a rule, credit-union savings are insured, dollar for dollar, up to a certain limit. Thus, a $2,000 account would be the equivalent of a paid-up $4,000 permanent life policy with a 50% cash value.

He would also be credited with an interest income on the $2,000, and the prevalent rate is currently 5%

Flunking a medical exam for life insurance given
by one company means that the information
about your physical inadequacies becomes available
to all life-insurance companies.

a year, compounded quarterly. That would give him
income of more than $100 a year, if he took the pay-
ment annually.

The one-for-one insurance ratio is reduced somewhat on savings deposited as the credit-union member advances in age, usually commencing at 55.

Other possible death benefits that can be obtained
without medical examination are certain travel-accident policies.

CHAPTER VIII

Frills,
Payments
and Dividends

When you enter an air terminal and see that pretty girl behind the flight-insurance counter, are you tempted to walk over to her? To draw her into conversation—about insurance?

What in this world could be more attractive than $7,500 of insurance for each quarter you plunk down? Right? Well, maybe. . . .

And, when you're talking about a new life-insurance policy (this time probably not to a pretty young girl), and your insurance agent suggests that you add the double-indemnity provision for a "nominal extra charge," do visions of dollar signs dance in your head? Could there be many better buys than this accidental

Flight insurance looks like too much of a bargain
to pass up. Statistically, however, it's not *that* good.

death benefit, which, for a few extra bucks a year, will give your wife and kids twice the face amount of the policy if you die accidentally? (Some companies sell triple indemnity.) Well. . . .

Low ticket items like double indemnity and flight insurance do attract a lot of people, many of whom buy them almost automatically. But a few hard questions should first be asked.

Are they worth the price?
Do you really need the additional insurance?

A bigger estate for an accident?

If you need the added protection, you and your family had better take another look at your insurance program. There is no sound reason why your family would need a bigger estate if you were to die accidentally rather than from natural causes. So it might be better to spend the money on expanding the family's basic program.

Of course, there are persons, particularly young people in excellent health, who are convinced that premature death would probably be accidental. They may have found statistics that they believe bolster this conclusion. Some may even decide that their business activity and avocational pursuits expose them to greater than normal risk of accidental death. In these cases, accidental-death benefits would appear to be in order.

There is not much we can say about this, except that it is difficult to build an estate plan on the premise that death will take a special form. What happens if the family's income producer reveals an uncooperative spirit by becoming ill and dying naturally? What value the accidental-death estate plan then?

There are persons who may be underinsured for medical, occupational or even financial reasons. They may feel that any bit of insurance from any source would be helpful. However, if the person is underinsured for financial reasons, he may find that the few dollars he spends here and there for bits of insurance may add up to enough to buy a small policy that would protect his family no matter what.

Anyone who travels extensively and decides that he wants the extra protection would probably be better off with a long-term travel-accident policy, rather than a string of short-term contracts.

There are persons who want the additional benefits offered by travel insurance and other accident policies. Many contracts pay not only in the event of death, but also if the insured person loses parts of his body or his sight. A person so disabled would find the extra money most helpful in his time of rehabilitation and readjustment. We will go no further with this subject, because disability insurance is not life insurance; anyway, we could not do full justice to the subject here.

A recommended disability benefit

Having said that, we now will talk about another disability benefit. This one, called the waiver-of-premium provision, may be bought as part of an ordinary life policy. It is a recommended feature. Under this provision, premiums that fall due after an insured person is deemed totally and permanently disabled would be waived. In effect, the insurance company would pay them. Disability must occur before you reach a certain age, usually 60, and disability must last at least six months before it will be considered permanent.

Some companies offer, at still higher cost, a disability provision that also would pay a monthly income if the insured person became totally and permanently disabled.

All companies give you the option of paying your life-insurance premiums annually, semiannually or, if the total bill is large enough, monthly. But bear in mind that the greater the frequency of payments, the greater the extra-service cost—up to 10% or more of the basic annual premium. Pay for each policy on an annual basis, if at all possible. If you have several policies, you may have each annual payment spaced so that the total cost of your life-insurance program need not be met within one brief period.

A good extra benefit to have on a life-insurance
policy is a waiver for disability: in effect, your premiums
are paid for you if you become disabled.

The increased administrative cost of spreading premium payments over the year makes it necessary for an insurance company to levy the extra charge. However, you could save that extra money by doing the same thing for yourself. You can set aside an appropriate amount in each budgetary period—weekly, biweekly or monthly—and have the total premium ready when it is due.

Through oversight, you may miss a premium due date. Should that happen, you would have a grace period as stated in your policy (sometimes up to 31 days) in which to make it up. If you are unable to do so, and your policy is a permanent one, you may take a premium loan against its cash value. Some policies, and yours may be one of them, have an automatic premium-loan provision. This provision can usually be added to a policy at no extra cost.

A choice of three

Should you decide not to continue the payments on your permanent policy, you would have a choice among three "nonforfeiture values." This is a far cry from the early days of life insurance in this country: then, anyone who stopped paying premiums on his life policy, thus letting it lapse, got nothing. This was called a "forfeiture." The more progressive companies later established nonforfeiture values for such a policyholder: some paid him cash, while others continued insurance protection beyond the date when he stopped paying premiums. The first state law giving policyholders a legal right to a nonforfeiture benefit was passed in Massachusetts in 1861. It granted an extended term insurance benefit, which stipulated minimum values that had to be provided upon termination of a policy that had been in force for a few years.

Cash, term or paid-up

Today, your three nonforfeiture values are as follows:

1) Cash value. When you let a policy lapse or surrender it, you are entitled to receive its cash value, less premium loans, if any. You may take this in a lump sum or as income.

2) Extended term insurance. This gives you the option of having continued protection in the amount of the original policy for as long a period as the net cash value can buy. This is stipulated in the contract.

3) Reduced paid-up insurance. This provision enables you to obtain a paid-up policy for a reduced amount of insurance, payable under the same conditions as your original permanent policy. If, for example, you have a whole-life policy, the paid-up insurance feature will protect you for life without

further premium payments, but the amount of the insurance is reduced. If you have an endowment policy, your reduced protection continues to the maturity date named in the original policy, at which time you will receive this reduced amount.

Every policy indicates which of these provisions would apply if your premium were overdue and you did not choose a nonforfeiture procedure within a given time. This would be 30, 60 or 90 days. Sometimes you will make this choice in your application for a policy. In some states, the law dictates which provision must take effect if the policyholder indicates no preference.

Your policy has one or more tables illustrating the nonforfeiture values. It also presents the mortality table and the rate of interest used in figuring the values. Values for years not shown in these tables may be obtained from your insurance company.

If your policy is a participating one you will be collecting dividends. Don't be misled into thinking these are like that cash income you may be receiving on some of the common stocks you own.

In the case of a participating policy, the premium is calculated so to allow some margin over the anticipated cost of protection and expenses. However, the actual yearly net cost of your insurance is determined only after the expenses, mortality losses and investment income of the company are known. Then you will receive partial refunds of the overcharges, usually after the first year or two. Being refunds, these are not viewed as income and are therefore not subject to taxation.

Devastating plagues, inaccurate tables

This procedure on dividends dates to the very early days of life insurance, when loss prediction was extremely difficult because of devastating plagues as well as very inaccurate mortality tables. The idea was to charge members of a mutual group just a bit more than might have been necessary, and divide up the surplus at year's end, if any money was left. If there was a deficit, the members were assessed to cover it.

The practice has been continued, but the vast majority of today's participating policies are not assessable. Considering the origin of the dividend plan you might conclude that participating policies are issued only by mutual companies, those nonprofit corporations technically owned by their policyholders. Not true. Participating policies also are issued by stockholder-owned companies, which also issue nonparticipating policies (without dividends) with premium rates set at lower levels than those of policies that pay dividends.

Why has the practice been continued? Partly because the unrefunded overpayments in the first year or two help to defray the high cost of acquiring business; partly because the overpayment-and-refund cycle provides an insurance company with more investment capital (an enlarged cash flow); and partly because people like to receive "dividends."

It's a good merchandising tool. But more than that, it is most beneficial to policyholders of companies that scrupulously increase the dividend rate as much as financial stability will allow as mortality losses and expenses decline and investment income rises.

How to treat dividends

As to what you should do with your dividends, you have four choices in all companies, and a fifth option in many. They are:

1) Take them in cash.

2) Use them to reduce premiums due.

3) Leave them with the company to accumulate at interest. You can always change your mind and take the cash when you want or need it. Make certain the interest rate you receive is competitive with that of banks, savings and loans and other thrift institutions.

4) Use them to buy additional paid-up permanent life insurance.

5) Appropriately, this is known as the "fifth dividend option," under which you may use the dividend

to buy one-year term insurance, usually up to the current cash value of the policy. It was designed primarily to offset policy loans made on the minimum-deposit purchase plan, which we looked into in an earlier chapter. Under that plan, generally advantageous only to persons in high tax brackets, policy loans are kept at the level of the increasing cash value, and the proceeds are used toward payment of the premiums.

Whatever dividend option you select, you usually can switch to another when it suits. Because of the strong desire to keep annual cash outlay as low as possible, many families find it most practical to take the dividends as credit in the payment of premiums.

CHAPTER IX

The Case
for
Wife Insurance

When Jim's wife died, the last thought that would have occurred to him in his hour of grief was that his emotional stress would be compounded by economic pressures.

At 37, he was earning $18,000 a year, and, while he and Marion had lived comfortably, they had been provident. They had been slowly building assets toward college for their children and for other long-term goals.

But after her death, Jim, with two daughters, 8 and 10, found himself in serious economic trouble. To keep his family together and living on the same standard they had been accustomed to, he found he was spending more than he was earning. Each month, he cut a little more deeply into his savings. How did this happen?

First, with Marion gone, someone had to run the house. So he hired a housekeeper at a cost of $75 a week, plus room and board. His friends assured him that he got a bargain, particularly in his area. Bargain or not, she cost him at least $5,000 a year, because she ate well, used the telephone and other utilities and added certain of her laundry costs to those of the family. In addition, she was not as conscientious a shopper as Marion had been, so Jim's costs went up generally on food, sundries and the children's clothing, some of which Marion used to make herself.

To have more time with the children, Jim hired workmen to do some of the jobs he used to tackle himself. There was the gardener, the local handyman, the house painter . . . and on and on, or so it seemed.

Jim hardly realized what was happening. It all came about so quickly. The sudden illness; the grief; the children's shock. The kids became so unmanageable, he could barely cope with them. What did money matter? The main objective was to get them—and himself—adjusted to their new life as quickly as possible. He couldn't think of adding to their emotional burden by taking them out of familiar surroundings: their home, their school, their friends, the helpful neighbors.

A widower with young children finds that while he
performs parental functions, he has to pay
professionals to do a lot of odd jobs he used to do himself.

And the money went.

Finally, Jim was forced to face economic reality.
Thorough analysis of his financial situation showed
that the extra expenses incurred since his wife's death
averaged about $510 a month, or $6,120 a year. From
that, he subtracted the $1,200 that had been his late
wife's average annual living expenses, and the $1,200
that had been saved in each of the last few years. He
next subtracted the $238 a month, or $2,856 a year,
the children received in Social Security survivors' ben-

efits under their mother's account as of the fall of 1972. (She had worked before they were born.)

The subtractions totaled $5,256, bringing his net extra cost to $864 a year, or $72 a month more than his take-home pay.

Jim took action to get the situation under control. He managed to shave his expenses by a bit more than $72 a month. He once again took on the gardening and other chores. And he imposed more stringent expense limits on the housekeeper, who fortunately was inclined to be helpful.

But that left him with no income for savings toward auto and appliance replacement and other short-term needs, let alone the bigger, long-term goals. And his savings were down by more than $3,000 in the year since his wife's death.

The extras were countless

Some $2,000 of that went toward medical and funeral costs, and the countless extras—restaurant meals, taxis, baby-sitters—that cropped up in that period of final illness and death.

Also spent then was the $2,000 in life insurance money that Jim had received. That $2,000 policy was all the insurance they had on Marion's life. They had discussed it several times, recognizing that costs would mount in her absence. At least once, they were on the verge of buying a low-cost policy. Jim remembered that.

"You'll remarry within the first year," a healthy and exuberant Marion had gibed, thus neatly closing the subject on several occasions. Jim remembered that, too.

To stay even, Jim took on free-lance work that occupied his evenings. With his job, the night work and his busy weekends as cook, gardener and handyman, he had minimal time with the children, but he tried to make the most of it. He had no time for himself.

Jim's life was not easy. He worked hard, and had little in the way of a social life, but he managed to keep his family together and regain a measure of contentment and economic security for them.

Jim's certainly was not the most difficult situation a widower has had to face. A man with less endurance or income, or both, might have had to reduce his family's living standards sharply. Worse yet, he might have had to break up his home and move in with relatives who could help care for the children. Other alternatives might be to take in a relative who would serve as housekeeper, or to enter into a hasty, "practical" marriage.

Tough choices.

That children are dependent on both their parents has been recognized by Congress. The legislators broadened the foundation for family security when they enacted the Social Security amendment that made children eligible for benefits when either parent (if he or she had worked) died, retired or became disabled. It became effective in February, 1968. It provided a considerably greater number of families with protection against the economic hardships of a wife's death.

Of course, before giving consideration to the purchase of life insurance on the wife and mother, the primary question always stands:

Does the father already have adequate insurance on his own life?

If he does, it must then be decided how much insurance would be needed to ease the economic burden of a wife's death. This would be accomplished by measuring each area of resulting economic loss and determining whether it could be comfortably absorbed by the family's income and assets.

The cost of replacing a mother's services could range from $1,200 to a startling $10,000 or more a year, depending on the family's economic status and the ages and degree of dependency of the children.

Wives in about a third of the nation's households have outside employment. In many of those homes, it may be considered vital to the family's financial program to replace at least part of the wife's earnings with insurance proceeds.

It is possible that a husband's loss of income-tax privileges at his wife's death may be large enough to warrant coverage. He would eventually lose his wife's personal exemption and the advantages of filing a joint return, but he would be allowed deductions from taxable income for the care of his children, up to $400 per month if his income was less than $18,000. And the reduced tax rates for a "head of household" make up in part for the loss of joint-return privileges.

A loss in Social Security

Another potential economic loss to a family without a mother is in Social Security benefits. If a widower with dependent children becomes permanently disabled or dies, benefits to his family may be reduced because of the absence of a wife. Their budgetary needs, meanwhile, would have already been swollen by the cost of replacing her essential services. At a widower's retirement at 65, the total Social Security benefits would be reduced by the amount his wife would have received. The family's monthly check would be cut by a third, for his wife would have received a monthly sum equal to half his retirement benefits.

Of interest to wealthier families would be the ultimate effect a wife's death could have on estate taxes. A major estate-tax advantage would be lost, for a surviving wife can claim a "marital deduction."

This would exempt up to 50% of her late husband's estate from taxes, provided that proper financial and legal precautions had been taken. (These will be discussed in another book in this series.)

For example, a $120,000 net estate left by a widower may be subject to a Federal estate tax of about $10,000. However, if there were a surviving spouse, and the marital deduction were taken, there would have been no tax liability.

A substantial tax burden

On the other hand, if a wife outlives her husband and is left with a large estate, the tax burden at her death might be substantial. For one thing, the marital deduction would not be available. Protection against this contingency also may be desired.

Once all applicable areas of potential economic loss from the wife's death have been evaluated, a family must measure the resultant needs. One will be for a lump sum, including an amount for final medical and funeral expenses, and perhaps for supplemental income for the children's dependent years. After estimating how much can be absorbed by income, savings, investments, Social Security benefits if any, and other assets, the family must decide how much it can afford for life insurance to cover the rest.

The allocation usually is small, so it may not be possible to do all that a family's survey recommends. To get the most protection for the money, it should concentrate on policies such as term, which has no cash value except in the case of death and, secondarily, whole life. Both policies stress protection more than savings. Also, there are combination family policies that offer low-cost protection for the wife and children, while putting primary insurance emphasis on the father.

Remember: Short-term needs, such as income for the children's growing years, should be covered by short-term policies. Don't carry more insurance than you need at any time.

CHAPTER X

The Case against Child Insurance

Over the years, the life-insurance industry has sharply reduced its field force of premium-collecting "debit men." These peripatetic salesmen covered urban neighborhoods, visiting families on a weekly or monthly basis to collect premiums on existing small policies and to sell new ones when some big family event took place.

The debit (or territory) men are a diminishing breed because, according to some big companies that have eliminated them completely, the more affluent public no longer wishes to buy "industrial" insurance, so called because it originally was sold primarily to factory workers.

The protection was in amounts under $1,000. A $250 policy might have cost as little as 25 cents a week, which the debit man would personally collect. That's $13 a year. So $1,000 of industrial life would have cost 4 times that, or about twice what comparable coverage would cost today for a 25-year-old man buying a $2,000 20-payment policy.

The debit man was around so frequently, usually once a week, he was often looked upon as a friend or advisor, almost like a member of the family. He instilled ideas about life insurance in the minds of people over several generations, and many of those ideas have filtered down, from parent to child to today's young adults. Some of the ideas were quite sound; others not so sound.

One of the sound ideas was that of striving for family economic security in the event of the death of the father, the chief income producer. However, these low-income people could not afford anywhere near the amount of protection they should have had. That made the debit man's sales job difficult. But the salesman had to earn a living, so he also pushed the sale of small policies on the lives of children, as they were born, generally catching the parents in a receptive, perhaps festive mood.

This, by and large, was not a sound idea.

The idea was not sound for a simple reason: the breadwinner had little insurance, if any at all, on his own life. And, as we soon shall see, it was not sound for other reasons. Even so, many young parents today, perhaps reaping thoughts sown by their own parents, insist on buying policies for their children.

Perhaps their feelings are the same as those of parents of yesteryear, who would almost automatically buy a $250 or $500 life policy on a newborn child. The few coins a week gave them the satisfaction of knowing they were doing "the right thing" by their kids. With the policy's cash-value build-up in mind, many bought it more as an enforced-savings device, as a "start" for their child, than as death protection. That the ultimate cash value often was considerably less than the total premiums paid didn't matter—or wasn't known.

As in the past, the vast majority of fathers carrying insurance on the lives of their children nowadays do not have enough on their own. Families may have larger incomes, but they are spending more, for today's higher living standards are more costly. This means that family heads must leave larger estates if they want their wives and children to continue living at more than a subsistence level, by today's standards, and to achieve educational and other goals.

Even when the father is adequately insured, it is not always wise to buy insurance on a child's life. Buying additional insurance on the father's life instead will satisfy many of the reasons for wanting juvenile insurance, while providing additional advantages.

Only a fraction of the cash value

At a father's death, insurance on his child's life naturally does not pay off. In fact, the child's policy may be discontinued unless the mother can continue paying the premiums, or unless the contract includes a "payor benefit." That benefit, obtained at extra cost, waives further premium payments if the payor dies before the child is 21. With this proviso, insurance on a child's life may mature or be paid up in time to provide cash for his college education or to finance some other special objectives. But cash may be needed sooner. An emergency may force surrender of the child's policy for its immediate cash value—at a fraction of its ultimate value.

Conversely, proceeds from a policy on the father are immediately available at his death. Even if the contract stipulates that payment be made by the insurance company at some future date—when the child is ready for college, for example—arrangements for emergency withdrawals would be possible before then. Furthermore, the money would be earning interest while in the custody of the insurance company.

A standard argument for child insurance states that if the father, for any reason, is uninsurable, then insurance must be taken out on the child's life. But now the question must be asked: What is the real goal? Is it savings? Or is it protection? If it is savings, then why buy a policy? What benefit would there be in a paid-up college fund at the insured child's premature death?

It would be far better to put the insurance-premium money into other much more productive investment and savings vehicles.

How to force yourself to save

If "enforced savings" is the attraction, a man could buy bonds through payroll deductions or make automatic deposits in a credit union or bank account. Or he could enter into a contractual plan that "obligates" him to invest monthly in a mutual fund, or he could use any of the other enforced-savings techniques available. He and his child would be ahead.

Of course, parents must place insurance on the child if they wish to cover medical and funeral expenses, which, in the case of a child's death, may run from a few hundred dollars to more than $1,000. The low-cost coverage afforded by a combination family-plan policy would serve adequately here, as explained in an earlier chapter.

An early start on a permanent plan

Another reason for taking out a policy on a child could be this: his parents or grandparents wish to start him on a permanent life-insurance program that he may take over when he is earning his own way. Advocates of this idea say that the child may be uninsurable for health or occupational reasons when he is older, and that his yearly cost when he takes over could be up to $5 less per $1,000 of protection than the going rate at his attained age. The older the buyer, the higher the insurance rates.

Opponents argue that the adult cost of a policy bought in childhood is lower only to the extent of its accumulated cash value. If the cash value of an old policy is 20% of the face, or protection, amount, then the cost is about 20% less than that of a new policy. Therefore, the early premium payments, these opponents argue, could have been more wisely invested and thus provide the child with an even bigger gift.

Understandably, life insurers wish to instill the virtues of their products in the minds of people early in their lives, so they have designed a number of policies specifically for parents and other relatives susceptible to the idea of starting a child's insurance program early. The concept is somewhat akin to establishment of a dowry, for the insured child-grown-older can present to his or her spouse a budding life-insurance program as a wedding gift.

The child-insurance concept is also said to help educate a child in the ways of prudent money management. That's unlikely: both the concept and the policy are remote to the child.

One special contract for child insurance is called the "jumping juvenile." This is usually sold in units that provide $1,000 of protection to age 21. Then the benefits automatically increase fivefold, with no premium increase or medical examination. The over-21 policy in this case is attractively priced; but the under-21 cost per year is high, giving only nominal protection for the money.

CHAPTER XI

Who Gets
the Money?
And How?

You know who you want to get your life-insurance money. To make certain your wishes are fulfilled, you must take precautionary steps. So the real question is: How do I make sure "they" get the money?

Before we get further into this, let's get a few definitions out of the way:

Give thought to naming the beneficiary of your life insurance,
and remember that you can name more than one:
your children as well as your wife, and perhaps a charity, too.

• Primary beneficiary: The person, persons or institution to whom the insurance proceeds will go when the insured person dies.

• Secondary beneficiary: The person, persons or institution to whom the balance of the insurance proceeds will go after the primary beneficiary's claim has been fulfilled or he dies. For example, the primary beneficiary (perhaps the widow) may receive the interest income from the insurance proceeds for life, with the principal then going to the secondary beneficiary (perhaps a child). You may have no need or desire to name secondary beneficiaries.

Parceling out the proceeds

• Contingent beneficiary: The person, persons or institution named in the policy to receive the insurance proceeds if the primary beneficiary, and secondary beneficiaries, if any, are dead when the insured person dies. Several contingent beneficiaries may be named in order, and the first survivor on the list would get the insurance proceeds. Or there may be a number of contingent beneficiaries, and the proceeds parceled out to them either in even shares or any other division you choose.

Ordinary life-insurance policies may be assigned to cover a debt or obligation. Unless you have retained the right to change the beneficiary, the beneficiary's consent to the assignment would be required.

If there are no living beneficiaries at your death, the proceeds would go into your estate.

> Too often people fail to make timely changes in their estate plans and about insurance beneficiaries as family changes take place. This can be especially true if tragedy strikes.

You have at your disposal the means with which to minimize that risk of negligence. For example, you may name your wife as primary beneficiary, and then name a number of contingent beneficiaries. Thus, if your wife died before you did, the first surviving contingent beneficiary, without need for further change in arrangements, would automatically receive the proceeds of the insurance.

Name the kids

The first contingent beneficiary you would probably name would be your children, listed as a group, who would share equally in the proceeds. Some policies automatically include children as contingent beneficiaries. If you have adopted children, it would be safest to name them specifically, or to stipulate that they have the same rights as your other children. If you were previously married, and want only the children of your present marriage to benefit, you must specify this.

Additional contingent beneficiaries may be other relatives of yours, close friends or perhaps a charity.

You can change your beneficiary arrangements if you had reserved the right to do so in your application for the policy. If you did not do so, then you must have your beneficiary's written consent before you can make the change. In certain circumstances, it may be wisest, if not necessary, that you name beneficiaries irrevocably, giving up the right to make changes.

If you choose to have your spouse, or other primary beneficiary, own your policy, you avoid having the value of your life-insurance proceeds included in your estate for estate-tax purposes. Insurance proceeds are not subject to income taxes and beneficiaries get them directly, but they are normally counted as part of the insured person's estate for tax purposes.

Farewell to "incidents of ownership"

To have the Internal Revenue Service accept your spouse (or other person) as the owner of your policy, you must give up all "incidents of ownership." The right to change beneficiaries is one of these "incidents." So is payment of premiums, which must be done by the owner. Even if a wife has no income of her own, the IRS recognizes her right to a part of her husband's income, with which she may do as she chooses. This can include paying for a life-insurance policy on her husband's life.

In this kind of estate planning you are getting yourself involved in tax-shelters, trusts and other arrangements designed to preserve more of your estate for your survivors. The going can get heavy. So it makes good sense to get the advice of both a lawyer and a tax consultant.

Bill and Grace, whom we met in Chapter I, decided that at his death she should receive all the proceeds on his policies in cash. The plan was to put that cash to work, providing supplemental income for her and the children, thus preserving the principal for later needs. Other choices were open to them, and in time their circumstances might change so much that they would reconsider the alternatives.

Stipulating the options

On your life insurance policies, you, like Bill and Grace, have the option of having your beneficiary receive the proceeds at your death in a lump sum, or as income under one of the alternatives known as "settlement options." These options are stipulated in your contracts. Under the terms of these options, the proceeds of your policy at maturity will be held by the insurance company, which will then begin paying a regular income in place of the lump-sum settlement. You may choose how the beneficiaries will get the money, or you may leave the choice of option to them.

There are three settlement options: interest payments; installment payments; annuity income for life. All but the very oldest ordinary-life policies offer these. If you have group-life insurance, you may choose an optional settlement provision by applying to your employer or writing to the insurance company that issued the coverage. (As a rule, optional settlements are not offered in industrial policies because of the small amount of insurance proceeds involved.)

Combining payment plans

Income-payment plans may be combined in different ways, if the proceeds are large enough to warrant this. Payments may be arranged on an annual, semiannual, quarterly or monthly basis. In most companies, each income payment must be for at least $10, and the policy proceeds must amount to at least $1,000.

Let's take a closer look at the settlement options:

• Interest payments: The money may be left with the insurance company until asked for by the beneficiary, who in the meantime would receive the interest it earns. This option is ordinarily not advisable, unless the interest rate is competitive with the rate paid by banks and other savings institutions. But check. Some insurance companies offer especially attractive interest rates if the money is left with them for a minimum period, usually two years.

This option could be useful to a family that needs time to select the best option for it, whether that be the cash lump-sum or an income plan. However, the interest-payment plan itself may be the final choice. The interest payments can be arranged to last for a specific number of years or for the recipient's life.

As a rule, it is also wise to set up the arrangement so that the beneficiary can make withdrawals from the principal for emergencies or special purposes.

Finally, arrangements can be made to have any remaining principal paid to some other person or an organization as beneficiary.

An interest-payment plan often is used to maintain a reserve fund, such as for children's educations, or when the money is to be passed to someone else at the death of the primary beneficiary, or at some predetermined time. For example, if Bill and Grace acquired sufficient wealth to leave Grace financially independent at his death, it perhaps would make sense to have her receive the interest income from the insurance proceeds for life, or until the children reach certain ages. They would then get the money directly, avoiding the possible tax costs of having it come to them through Grace's estate.

• Installment payments: These can be arranged in either of two ways. Monthly installments of a specific amount may be paid until the insurance proceeds and interest have been exhausted. Or monthly income may be paid over a given period of time, using up principal and interest in that period.

Paying on the installment plan

If you select the installment payment plan for your beneficiary, you may choose to permit him or her to commute the remaining payments, that is, stop income payments and take all the money that remains in one final lump sum. On the other hand, you can arrange to have the money left when the primary beneficiary dies paid in a lump sum or as income to one or more secondary beneficiaries.

• Life annuity income: A life annuity pays a specific income regularly to the annuitant (in this discussion, the beneficiary) for as long as he or she lives. Obviously, the amount paid monthly on a given policy will be smaller if the beneficiary is young and likely to collect for a long time, and larger if he is older.

Reduced lifetime income may be taken in exchange for a guarantee by the insurance company that payments will continue to be made to another person if the annuitant dies before the payments total a certain amount, or before they have been paid for a certain length of time. The arrangement under the provision for a minimum number of payment years might, for example, be for "10-years certain" or "20-years certain." If the primary beneficiary (the annuitant) dies within that period, or before his payments total the certain amount, a named contingent beneficiary would receive the balance of the income, either in installments or in the immediate-cash equivalent.

Yours may be one of the many policies that allows the choice of a "joint and survivor" life annuity as an income settlement. Two persons would receive the income jointly. Upon the death of one, the survivor would continue to receive either the same income for life, or two-thirds of the amount, depending on the wording of the provision.

An annuity-income settlement may be the choice of an insured person who is convinced that his beneficiary would not be capable of managing a large sum of money, and that a competent money manager, or investment counselor, could not be engaged. Even if a competent investment counselor could be found, the fact that the beneficiary would have access to the principal investment sum might disturb the insured.

A prudent man might decide that his beneficiary
would go berserk with a lump-sum payment of life-insurance
proceeds and therefore stipulate that he will not get a lump sum.

CHAPTER XII

Charitable Giving and Other Tax Advantages

Exploring the ways in which life insurance can be used as a vehicle for philanthropy reveals that generosity can be made to pay off handsomely—for the donor as well as for the recipient—and not in spiritual uplift alone, but also in cash in the form of tax savings.

The basic mechanism is simple: a donor names his college, his church, a hospital or other favorite institution as the beneficiary in a new or existing insurance policy on his life. The designation must be irrevocable so he cannot name another beneficiary later, after having enjoyed a tax advantage. If the policy is one he has owned for a while, the donor may claim its cash value as a deduction from taxable income on his federal income-tax return. Whether the policy is old or new, he may also deduct his premium payments each year.

Anyone in a low or moderate income-tax bracket would find the tax advantage limited, or perhaps even nonexistent. The premium payments would be part of whatever total amount of charitable contributions he would normally deduct each year anyhow. And at his death, there probably would be no major estate-tax problem.

The satisfaction of giving

But even a low- or moderate-income donor could find satisfaction in giving through life insurance, for he would know that his philanthropic goal would be completed whether he lived or died. Furthermore, the total gift would ultimately be greater, in all probability, than what he would have been able to afford otherwise.

An illustration of this was presented in a fund-raising brochure of a nonprofit organization. A 35-year-old man wishing to give $2,000 to

Not only can you get a glow of well doing by giving to
non-profit organizations through the medium of
a life-insurance policy, you can get tax and estate savings also.

that institution could buy a 20-payment, whole-life policy that would cost some $1,380 over the 20 years, or about $69 a year. At his death, the organization would receive $2,000, $620 more than he had paid for the gift, even without any tax savings.

The greatest harvest of tax savings through use of life insurance for charitable contributions is reaped by people with big incomes and, in the case of estate-tax benefits, people of wealth. Suppose, for example, you could see that you would leave an estate of $1 million when you died. You direct some of your current charitable giving to the purchase of a $500,000 policy for the benefit of a charity.

The premiums become deductible

An immediate benefit to you, of course, is that you can deduct the premiums from your taxable income. You name the recipient institution irrevocable beneficiary and, if you like, the owner of the policy. However, you retain an "incident of ownership," such as the right to decide how the beneficiary will ultimately receive the proceeds of the insurance. This allows the policy's proceeds to be included in your estate at your death, bringing the total up to $1.5 million.

What would otherwise happen to your estate of $1 million without the big gift? It would become an

adjusted gross estate of perhaps $900,000 after deduc-
tion of about $100,000 in expenses. If your will had
been properly drawn, your widow would be entitled
to half that gross, tax-free, as her marital deduction.
The remainder would be further reduced by the
standard $60,000 deduction for the deceased, leaving
a taxable balance of $390,000. The federal estate tax
on that amount, not considering any credit for state-
tax payments, would be $110,500.

Mixed feelings at charitable institutions

How does the $1.5 million estate, including the
$500,000 charitable policy, fare? The adjusted gross
estate would be $1.4 million, allowing for the same
$100,000 in permissible expenses. Your widow's tax-
free marital deduction would be half that gross, or
$700,000. Of the balance, $500,000 (the proceeds of
the policy) would go, tax-free, to the institution you
named in the policy, leaving $200,000 from which the
deceased's personal deduction of $60,000 would be
made. The $140,000 remainder would be the taxable
balance on which a federal estate-tax payment of
$32,700 would be due. The tax saving: $77,800.

There are mixed feelings about these insur-
ance-giving plans at some charitable institutions. And there are some disadvantages for
charities in them. The assumption is that con-

tributors would reduce their cash gifts, at least in part, by the amounts they pay in insurance premiums. Could the institution concerned survive on less current cash income?

Here's an illustration. A 50-year-old man who gives $4,000 a year to his church could buy up to $100,000 of straight-life insurance with that amount. In direct

Charitable institutions are not always happy to see gift-giving deferred in the form of life-insurance policies: they always need cash now as well as later.

payments to the institution, it would take him 25 years to give a total of $100,000, and statistically, he's not likely to live that long, so the policy would guarantee that the church ultimately would get a much larger sum. But could the church manage in the meantime without the annual $4,000 income?

Not all of the current income need be sacrificed, of course.

Most charitable insurance programs are built on so-called permanent insurance. If the beneficiary institution is also the owner of the policy, two economic opportunities are available to it. As we have seen, permanent insurance builds cash values, and the institution could borrow against them or use them as collateral for other loans. In addition, if dividends are paid, as they are on participating policies, the institution could take these as income. In the case of the $100,000 policy taken by the 50-year-old man, the dividends could amount to $400 to $600 in the second year and grow to $1,200 by the 15th year, provided that the dividend scale holds firm.

They prefer the cash

But several representatives of charitable organizations have voiced the view that these current cash advantages probably are not enough to affect the loss of full annual income. They tend to agree that life-insurance programs should be only a part of fund-raising efforts. They apparently prefer separate, supplemental insurance plans that do not reduce the regular yearly income from cash contributions.

For special situations spanning a fixed period of time, term insurance, with small cash outlays, can be used. This is pure death protection that generally does not accumulate cash values, but it can be useful to an institution. For example, a few persons might take large term policies on their lives to cover a major loan that a school has taken out, with the idea of repaying it in a given number of years.

Another aspect of life insurance and taxes can be profitably discussed here even though it is not connected to charitable giving. This has to do with diminishing the tax bite on insurance proceeds.

We have noted previously that life-insurance proceeds go directly to the beneficiary. This avoids the delays and costs of processing through probate court. However, insurance proceeds are counted as part of the insured person's total estate for tax purposes.

Transferring ownership

The risk of a possible estate-tax bite—of perhaps a bigger bite than necessary—can be avoided by transferring ownership of insurance policies to the beneficiary or any other person. If you choose to do this, to make the transfer of ownership valid in the eyes of the Internal Revenue Service, you cannot retain any incidents of ownership. You give up, irrevocably, all rights of ownership of the contracts: you

cannot change the beneficiary, decide how he or she would receive the money at your death, borrow on the cash values, use the policy as collateral for other loans, assign the policy or pay the premiums.

If a wife thus becomes the owner of life-insurance policies, and she is not employed and has no separate income, she still can pay the premiums with her share of her husband's income, as noted previously.

DoTy

A way to avoid heavy estate taxes is to give ownership
of a life-insurance policy to the beneficiary now.

No question of gift tax is involved if the beneficiary
becomes the owner of a new policy which at that
point has no cash value. But if you pass ownership of
an existing permanent policy that has accumulated
cash value, you may be subject to a federal gift tax.

However, gift-tax rates are lower than estate-tax
charges, and tax-free gifts are allowed up to certain
limits. A person may give up to $3,000 a year to each
of as many persons as he wishes without being sub-

ject to a gift tax. In addition, he has the right, during his lifetime, to give $60,000 to his spouse or $30,000 to someone else without paying a gift tax. The real value of most property that people will pass during their lifetime to relatives and close friends will be within these limits. So, in most cases, both gift and estate taxes would be avoided by transferring ownership of an insurance policy to a beneficiary.

Although life-insurance death payments are not subject to income taxes, if the proceeds are taken as income rather than as a lump sum, there will be some interest payment in each installment received. The portion that represents interest is subject to taxation.

When a policyholder receives benefits from his own life insurance (one company refers to these benefits as "living benefits"), the proceeds are occasionally larger than the amount he has paid in premiums. The difference is regarded as taxable income.

CHAPTER XIII

Life Insurance for Business Purposes

Some 70% of all the organizations engaged in manufacturing, wholesale, retail and service operations in the US are sole proprietorships. Other small firms are partnerships and closely held corporations. All told, the nation's small businesses number in the many hundreds of thousands.

A small businessman realizes that he must acquire the fringe benefits that he might otherwise have received as an employee of a larger company. These include group health and life insurance, sick leave, vacations, retirement income and so on.

But there is another contingency-planning provision that is often overlooked. This is the provision for continuance of the business after the death of one of its principals. That, of course, would be the owner if the business is a sole proprietorship, or one of the partners or principals of a partnership or small corporation.

A properly drawn and implemented plan for business continuity would make life a lot less difficult for the surviving principals, while assuring that the interests of the deceased principal's family are protected.

The instrument for this purpose is known as business life insurance.

There are no basic differences between business life and the life insurance you buy for personal and family needs. Personal and family needs are broader, and perhaps include financial protection against disability and arrangements for income at retirement. On the other hand, the protection formulated for business concerns involves many more complex details to meet legal, financial, tax and technical problems.

These are the primary purposes of business life insurance, as set forth by the Institute of Life Insurance:

• Key-man protection: to compensate for the loss of

A partnership that has not invested in business
life insurance can be in trouble when a partner goes.

an essential employee or to pay for a replacement.

• Partnership insurance: to finance purchase of a deceased partner's interest by the surviving partner or partners.

• Corporation insurance: to finance the company's purchase of a major shareholder's interest at his death.

• Proprietorship insurance: to provide for maintenance of a business upon the death of the sole owner.

• Credit stabilization: insurance used to bolster a company's credit status, covering the owner or key man during the period of a loan or the duration of a mortgage on its property.

• Estate protection: insurance on a man's life if his estate consists almost entirely of his interest in a business. Payable to his family at his death, the proceeds provide them with immediate cash and thus allow them time to dispose of his interest in the business.

Whatever the structure of a business, the contingency problems cannot normally be solved simply by the purchase of some life insurance. That step should be an outgrowth of careful planning. Because a major part of that planning involves funding—i.e., creating a sum of money for a specific purpose—and because most small businessmen have limited capital for that purpose, life insurance is generally depended on for this.

As the first step in planning, the principal or principals should consult with the company's lawyer, accountant, bank trust-officer and life-insurance agent. While the first three can provide the basic information on which the plan can be built, the insurance agent can give technical advice concerning the type and arrangement of policies.

Among the planning considerations, naturally, are income- and estate-tax factors, with the natural objective of keeping them at a minimum.

Let's examine more closely the purposes to which business life insurance can be put.

Insuring know-how

• Key-man protection: Even a relatively small business may have one or more persons upon whom it counts rather heavily for its success. That person may of course be the owner. Or the manager. Or he could be the financial man, with responsibility for the company's credit standing, and for arranging new financing and short-term credit needs. It might be the sales manager or, if it's a retail store, the top salesman or the buyer. It might be an engineer, a chemist or other technician or scientist whose know-how is vital to a manufacturing company's success.

If there is any person whose death would destroy a business, or at the very least set it back until a replacement is functioning, then key-

If a business depends heavily on one man's talents, it makes sense to take out a "key man" life-insurance policy on him.

man insurance is probably needed. It provides benefits at the death of this vital employee, so that the company will have the resources with which to employ and train a successor and to offset the possible loss of profit in the mean-time.

• Partnership insurance: If the business is a partnership, special survivorship problems must be considered. Because a partnership is dissolved by the death of a partner, either at once or shortly thereafter, death poses a serious threat to the continuity of the business, and constitutes a hazard to the interests of the surviving partners and their late partner's heirs.

How a partnership is affected by a partner's death depends on the terms of the partnership agreement. As a rule, normal partnership operation ends at that time and the surviving partners become "liquidating trustees," confined to closing out the affairs of the partnership. If they continue the business, they may become personally liable for all losses or, in some states, for losses in excess of the value of the partnership's assets.

An accounting for the heirs

The dead partner's heirs cannot legally enter the business or take over his share. But they can demand an accounting and then a cash settlement of their share of the firm's net worth.

Controversy over the value of a deceased partner's interest can result in protracted litigation that would effectively freeze the business. There are several ways to avoid this kind of difficulty. One is an adequately financed buy-and-sell agreement. It would provide for the purchase by the heirs at a prearranged valuation of the deceased partner's interest. Legal documents must be drawn up in advance to state the terms of any such agreement.

If a buy-and-sell agreement is decided upon, the next stop is to fund the arrangement, and that can be done with the proceeds from business life insurance. Funding enables the surviving partners to reorganize at once and continue in business. It liquidates the interest of the deceased partner without loss. It enables

the heirs of the deceased partner to secure full value for his interest in the firm, at once and with a minimum of difficulty. Finally, it helps to sustain the credit standing of the firm.

How to establish a partnership-insurance plan? One way is to have each partner buy policies on the lives of the other partners. If there are three or more partners, the firm might buy a policy on the life of each partner.

Many questions are involved and answers must be devised. Among them: How much premium should

A firm with a number of top men does well to insure the lives of all of them for the benefit of the firm—and the survivors.

each partner pay? How much insurance is needed? What beneficiary arrangements and policy assignments are necessary? What will the tax effects be?

Valuation of the partnership is one of the most vital, complex and troublesome of the problems to be met in setting up a partnership-insurance plan. The reason: an attempt is being made now to set up a formula that will give full value to a deceased partner's heirs in the future. But the determination cannot be put off until that future time, because it would be even more difficult then, with the dead partner's heirs possibly fighting for a settlement based on exaggerated valuation of his share.

The simplest basis of valuation is to set, in advance, an arbitrary value on each partner's interest. This method avoids arguments later, but it makes no provision for the possibility of a rapid shift in value through growth of the business. The formula used can include a fixed value for goodwill and the net book value, calculated by subtracting liabilities from current asset value. Goodwill is the element most difficult to measure, and it is here that controversy is most likely to start.

The plan can include a procedure that would periodically allow the partners to agree on a revised valuation. Another possibility is to leave valuation to a trustee or to later arbitration under a stipulated arbitration plan.

It is important to have all business, legal, financial and insurance needs and facilities carefully evaluated by experts. The ultimate plan should be the most effective and economical they can devise. This is especially important in a partnership, because there is little time in which to move after a principal's death.

A perpetual "legal person"

• Corporation insurance: This is of special concern to the small corporation with a few shareholders who are close to the management of the business. Ownership and management, in fact, are frequently the same. Most of the nation's corporations are of this type, for many small, closely held businesses have adopted the corporate form primarily for its legal, tax and other benefits. Unlike a partnership, a corporation is not terminated at the death of an owner: it is a legal "person," and its life is perpetual.

However, while a corporation is not as directly and immediately affected by the death of a principal as is a partnership, unfortunate consequences might follow. A deceased major stockholder's shares may be transferred to a person unknown to the management, and this could be disruptive. The new owner, for example, may choose to take the same active role performed by the late stockholder, though he may not be qualified to do so. The result: management and personal clashes that might seriously affect the corporation through impairment of credit, loss of business or damage to employee morale.

An heir to shares of stock in a company may not be qualified to exercise the rights that ownership of those shares confers on him.

Unless otherwise arranged, the deceased stock-holder's shares become part of his estate and pass into the hands of its executor or adminis-trator during the period of its settlement. He can vote the stock. If it is a controlling interest, he can name a new board of directors and take full control of the company.

How to avoid these pitfalls? One way is an ade-quately financed stock-sale-and-purchase agreement. It is comparable to the partnership buy-and-sell agreement, and it, too, can be funded by insurance. An effective corporation insurance program on the lives of principal stockholders would provide the company with the funds necessary to buy up and re-tire a deceased stockholder's interest. In doing so, the company gives the deceased stockholder's heirs full value for his interest at once. Thus the shock of changes in ownership are reduced, if not eliminated.

What's fair market value?

Here, too, an effective valuation formula is essen-tial. Most small, closely held corporations have no outside stockholders. With no public ownership of the stock, there is no public trading and, therefore, no "fair market value" set on its shares. As in the case of the partnership, the corporation's valuation for-mula would have to go beyond the book, or net asset, value of its shares. The formula would also have to take into consideration the company's goodwill.

• Individual proprietorship insurance: As has been noted, the majority of the nation's businesses are of the type owned and managed by one person. The death of an individual proprietor presents its own special business and estate problems.

Most state laws stipulate that upon the death of a sole proprietor, his business becomes part of his estate. The business is to be administered by his executor or administrator and passed to the heirs as quickly as possible, unless other provisions had been made.

In short, the heirs of the owner of a one-man business face the possibility of a loss, or even liquidation at a severe sacrifice, unless a specific plan has been set up in advance to assure continuity of the business, if that is the wish of the heirs.

Incidentally, a sole proprietorship also faces the possibility of loss to the firm even before his death, i.e., if he is disabled and incapable of participating in the business.

Upon the death of a proprietor, the business may be left to a relative or other heir, sold to the employees, sold to outsiders, continued by the trustees or executors, or liquidated. Any of these choices, unless formulated under a carefully-drawn plan, can generate problems for the sole proprietor's heirs. A sale might be forced either by the need for cash or by the demands of heirs, and a forced sale can frequently result in severe losses.

If the executor takes over the business, he probably must employ a manager. The manager would know, among other things, that the work was temporary, and he just might not do the best job possible. Any abnormality in operations of the business can disturb customer goodwill and employee morale. Credit problems also can arise.

If the son or other heir inherits the business, he might not be qualified. He might even still be a minor at the proprietor's death. Or he might have conflicts with other heirs, or with the employees. Or he might be hamstrung by insufficient working capital or credit.

If the business is transferred to employees or outsiders, there may be controversy over valuation. Or funds to complete the transaction may be lacking. Administrative delays, even when a will exists, can cause serious losses.

Whatever the plan for the disposal or continuance of the business, funds will be needed. There will be debts, taxes and administrative costs, and the family may require income.

If the family is to continue the business after the estate is settled, it may be necessary to employ a manager, and working capital will probably be needed, at least for the readjustment pe-

An important shareholder-by-inheritance may be not quite mature enough to take his father's place in the company.

riod. If employees are to take over, funds for their purchase of the business probably would have to be made available, at least in part. If the business is to be sold, working capital will be needed for a transition period, and perhaps for the possible discounting of assets that often accompanies such a sale.

The funding, of course, can be accomplished with business life insurance, the amount and type to be dictated by the proprietor's program, carefully worked out in consultation with his lawyer, accountant, banker and life-insurance agent. The plan should include a will covering disposition of the business, a purchase-and-sale agreement or other plan for the disposal or continuation of the business, and an estimate of the funds required to execute the plan.

If the proprietor wishes to have the business sold to his employees at his death, he may consider the advantages of combining a pension or profit-sharing plan with a purchase agreement. It could be funded by insurance on the life of the owner, as is the case, of course, with all insurance bought to fund the disposition of a one-man business.

Permanent or other?

• Types of insurance: Many insurance men and other experts emphasize the use of so-called permanent policies—those that build cash values—in business-life-insurance funding plans. One advantage of these policies is that the cash values become assets of the business, and they may be borrowed against in times of need.

However, the premium outlay for permanent policies is relatively large, especially when compared with the cost of term life insurance which generally has no cash-value build-up. Some experts advocate the use of term insurance exclusively, on the grounds that any expenditure above the low cost of term insurance is a poor investment.

It is sound practice to split the money you have available for life insurance between term and a form of permanent insurance.

Arguments for and against term or permanent insurance are of little concern to the man who can afford only a term policy. If that is the only coverage he can buy, it is the one he should be happy to settle on, and the one his agent should urge him to settle on.

Here is an example of what can happen:

Mike and Sid were partners in a stationery store. They carried business life insurance for the first two difficult years of operation. But it was high-premium, permanent insurance, and they felt they could not afford to continue it. Besides, both partners were young, so how great was the risk? They dropped the policy.

When Mike died at 39, they had no coverage at all. His wife attempted to take his place, but she was not qualified, and did not get along with Sid. Furthermore, she was not able to give full attention to her young children. The result, after much aggravation, was sale of the business at a sacrifice price.

If Mike and Sid had been sold a low-outlay term policy, they might have had the protection when it was needed.

A final word about business life insurance:

Once established, the plan should be reviewed periodically, perhaps yearly, by experts, so that it is kept in tune with any changes in valuation, tax laws and other variable factors.

APPENDIX

GLOSSARY

A

accidental death benefit
A provision added to an insurance policy for payment of additional money in case of death by accidental means. The increase in benefits might be two or three times the amount of protection stated in the basic policy. Often referred to as "double indemnity."

actuary
Someone with professional training in the technical aspects of insurance, particularly the mathematical.

agent
A sales and service representative of an insurance company. A life insurance agent may also be called "a life underwriter."

annuity
An income provided by contract for a specified period of time, such as a number of years, or for life, in return for payment of premiums over a stated period.

application
A statement of information made by a person in applying for life insurance. It is used by the insurance company to determine the acceptability of the risk and the basis of the policy contract.

assignment of policy
The legal transfer of ownership of a policy from one person to another.

automatic premium loan
A provision in a life insurance policy authorizing the company automatically to pay (by means of a loan on the policy) any premium not paid by the insured when due.

B

beneficiary
The person named in a policy to receive the money, or proceeds, on the death of the insured person.

business life insurance
Insurance bought by a business enterprise on the life of one or more of its members. It is often bought by partnerships to protect the surviving partners against economic loss caused by the death of a partner, or by a corporation to reimburse it for loss caused by the death of a key employee.

C

cash (surrender) value
The money a policyholder gets back if he gives up a "permanent" policy, i.e., one that accrues cash value as premiums are paid on it, before it becomes payable at death or maturity. Also, what a life-insurance policy is worth as collateral for a loan.

claim
Notification made to an insurance company that payment of a specified amount is due under the terms of a life insurance policy.

commuted value
Immediate cash that would be available to a beneficiary in lieu of predetermined monthly installment payments of insurance proceeds. For example, a beneficiary may elect to take $15,800 in cash rather than payments of $100 monthly over 20 years—$24,000—under a family-income plan.

contingent beneficiary
The person named in the policy to receive the proceeds of a policy if the primary beneficiary is already dead when the insured person dies. Several contingent beneficiaries may be named, and the first survivor on the list would get the money.

convertible term insurance
Term insurance that can be exchanged, at the option of the policyholder and without having to prove insurability, for another plan of insurance.

credit life insurance
Term life insurance issued through a lender or lending agency to cover payment of a loan, installment purchase or other obligation in case of death.

D

decreasing-term insurance
A term policy on which the face amount gradually declines, eventually reaching zero at the end of the insurance period.

disability benefit
A provision added to a life insurance policy that goes into effect if the insured becomes totally and permanently disabled. It calls for the company to waive, or cancel, premium payments. Sometimes the company also undertakes to pay a monthly income to the insured.

dividend
Refund of premium overpayment on a participating policy. Being a refund and not a profit, it is not taxable. It cannot be guaranteed, because it depends on the insurance company's operating results.

dividend addition
An amount of paid-up insurance automatically bought with a dividend that has become due on a policy and is added to the face amount of the policy.

dividend options
How to use the dividends on a mutual insurance company policy, or on a special policy from nonmutual companies. 1) The dividends can be taken in cash. 2) They can be used to reduce premium payments. 3) They can be left with the company to earn interest. 4) They can be used to buy additional paid-up insurance. 5)

They can be used to purchase, automatically and annually, one year of term insurance equal to the cash value of the policy at that time.

double indemnity
See accidental death benefit.

E

endowment insurance
Insurance payable to the insured if he is living on the maturity date stated in the policy, or to a beneficiary if the insured dies prior to that date.

extended term insurance
A form of insurance available as a "nonforfeiture option." It provides the original amount of insurance for a limited period of time, even if premium payments are discontinued.

F

face amount
The sum that will be paid on death of the insured person or at maturity of the contract. It is stated on the "face" of the policy. It does not include dividend additions or additional amounts payable under accidental death or other special provisions.

family-income policy
A life-insurance policy, combining whole life and decreasing-term insurance, under which the beneficiary receives income payments for a specified period of years, if the insured person dies before the end of that period. The face amount is paid to the beneficiary either at the end of the period or at the death of the insured. Sometimes an option is open to the beneficiary allowing him to take, instead of the income payments, additional immediate cash equal to the commuted value of the total income payments.

family policy
A life insurance policy providing protection on the lives of all or several family members in one contract. Generally it takes the form of whole-life insurance on the husband and smaller amounts of term insurance on the wife and children, including those born after the policy is issued.

fifth dividend option
The right to use the dividends on a policy issued by a mutual insurance company (or on a special policy from other companies) to purchase, automatically and annually, one year of term insurance equivalent to the policy's cash value at that time. No physical examination is required.

fraternal life insurance
Protection provided by fraternal orders or societies to their members.

G

grace period
Usually 30 or 31 days after the date the premium is due, during which an overdue premium may be paid without penalty. The policy remains in force during this period.

group-life insurance
Life insurance issued, usually without medical examination, on a group of persons under a single master policy. It usually is issued to an employer for the benefit of his employees. The individual members of the group hold certificates stating what their coverage is.

I

industrial life insurance
Insurance sold in amounts under $1,000—more usually under $500—by debit men, or insurance agents with sales territories, who personally collect the premiums weekly or monthly. This kind of coverage, which has declined in popularity, got its name because it was born a century ago, in the early days of the industrial revolution, and was sold mainly to factory workers. It is expensive because of high administrative costs.

insured, the
The person on whose life a policy is issued.

L

lapsed policy
A policy terminated for nonpayment of premiums. The phrase is sometimes limited to a termination occurring before the policy has a cash or other surrender value.

legal reserve life insurance company
A company operating under state insurance laws which specify the minimum reserves the company must maintain on the policies it sells.

level-premium insurance
The cost of this insurance is distributed evenly over the period during which premiums are paid. Because the premium remains the same from year to year, it is much more than the actual cost of protection in the earlier years and much less in the later years, when the chance of death is statistically greater. The overpayments in the early years build up the reserve, or cash value, which is, in effect, included in the face amount paid on death.

limited payment life insurance
Whole-life insurance on which premiums are payable for a specified number of years, or to a certain age (such as 60) or until death, if death occurs before the end of the specified period. Or a contract may call for the insurance to be paid-up at a certain age of the insured, say, 60.

M

maturity date
The date on which an endowment policy begins to pay

benefits to its owner. If the insured has died before then, the beneficiary receives the face amount.

mortality tables
Tabular expressions of the death rate for various ages, usually expressed in terms of so many per thousand.

mutual life insurance company
A nonprofit corporation that is technically owned by its policyholders. However, though sometimes invited, the policyholders generally do not attend annual meetings, do not elect directors and officers and have little or no say about their company's operation. These companies usually issue participating policies.

N

nonforfeiture option
One of the choices available to a policyholder who chooses to discontinue the required premium payments. The policy value, if any, may be taken in cash, as extended term in-surance or as reduced paid-up insurance.

nonparticipating policy
A life insurance contract on which the premium covers the anticipated cost of insurance protection and related expenses and also allows for a profit for the company. No dividends are paid. "Nonpar" policies are issued by profit-motivated stockholder-owned life companies, many of which also sell participating policies —for reasons noted below. See participating policy.

O

options
Clauses in life insurance policies which allow the policyholder to choose additional coverage, e.g., double indemnity; or to choose between various alternatives, e.g., how to handle dividends.

ordinary life insurance
Coverage usually issued in amounts of $1,000 or more with premiums payable on an annual, semiannual, quarterly, or monthly basis. The term is also used as a synonym for "straight life insurance."

P

paid-up insurance or paid-up policy
Insurance on which all required premium payments have been made. A paid-up contract cannot be surrendered for the full face amount, but only for its cash value, which may be no more than two-thirds of the face amount. By contrast, a paid-up endowment is "mature," or has matured, and pays the face amount.

participating policy
A contract on which the premium is calculated to allow some margin over the anticipated cost of protection plus expenses. After the first year or two, the policyholder usually receives partial refunds of those overcharges in the form of so-called dividends.

permanent-life insurance
A phrase used to cover any form of life insurance except term, i.e., insurance that generally accrues cash value.

policy loan
A loan made by an insurance company to a policyholder, with his policy's cash value as security. The insurance protection is reduced by the amount of the loan until the loan is repaid. The most prevalent interest rate, stipulated in the contract, is an attractive 5%, though this has been increased on newer policies issued in many states.

preauthorized check plan
A plan by which a policyholder arranges with his bank and insurance company to have his premium payments drawn from his checking account, usually monthly.

premium
The payment, or one of the periodic payments, a policy owner agrees to make for an insurance policy.

premium loan
A loan made against a policy to pay the premium.

proceeds
The money paid on a life insurance policy after the death of the insured or when the maturity date has been reached.

R

renewable term insurance
Term insurance that can be renewed at the end of the term, at the option of the policyholder and without evidence of insurability, for a limited number of successive terms. The rates increase at each renewal as the age of the insured increases.

revival
The reinstatement of a lapsed policy by the company upon receipt of evidence of insurability and payment of past-due premiums, with interest.

S

settlement option
One of the ways in which the

policyholder or beneficiary may choose to have the proceeds of a policy paid. This may be done in the form of a lump sum or through various income plans.

stock life insurance company
A company owned by stockholders who elect a board to direct the company's management. *See* participating policy.

straight life insurance
Whole-life insurance on which premiums are payable during the life of the insured. This insurance has a cash-value build-up.

supplementary contract
An agreement between a life insurance company and a policyholder or beneficiary by which the company retains the cash sum payable under an insurance policy and makes payments in accordance with the settlement option chosen.

surrender value
What a policy is worth in cash when given up by the policyholder. Also known as cash value.

T

term insurance
Insurance payable to a beneficiary at the death of the insured, provided death occurs within a specified period, such as 5 or 10 years, or before a specified age. In its purest form, it is simple death protection, with no cash-value build-up.

U

underwriting
The process by which an insurance company determines whether or not and on what basis it will accept an application for insurance.

W

waiver of premium
See disability benefit

whole-life insurance
Insurance payable to a beneficiary at the death of the insured. Premiums may be payable for a specified number of years (limited-payment life) or for life (straight life). This insurance has a cash-value build-up in addition to providing death protection.

THE TOP 100 COMPANIES
BY CATEGORY

There are nearly 2,000 companies in the US that sell life insurance and they vary enormously in three important categories: the amount of insurance written the previous year; the total amount of insurance in force at that time; and the total assets. The following pages rank the leading 100 companies according to those three categories as they stood in 1971 and in earlier years, in order to give some estimation of growth patterns.

In making up a life-insurance program, as outlined in *Making Your Life Insurance Work For You,* you need to consider not only your own needs and goals and available funds, but also the agent and the company or companies he represents.

These tabulations come from *Best's Review,* the leading life-insurance trade journal.

Asterisks indicate mutual life-insurance companies. These offer participating policies on which so-called dividends are paid.

The top 100 life-insurance companies
ranked by insurance issued in 1971

Rank 1971	Company	Written in 1971	% Incr. over 1970	Rank 1971	Company	Written in 1971	% Incr. over 1970
1	Prudential*	$17,688,808,175	5.1	51	Home Life, N.Y.* ...	951,196,399	7.8
2	Metropolitan Life* ..	16,541,035,650	9.5	52	No. Amer. Life, Can.*	926,734,023	20.7
3	Equitable Society* ..	8,404,575,388	39.6	53	Puritan Life	919,988,579	-6.7
4	John Hancock*	8,157,400,021	-2.6	54	General American* .	908,486,814	-10.1
5	New York Life*	7,082,877,845	.6	55	State Mutual*	850,190,985	-15.1
6	Old Republic Life ...	6,798,235,536	11.7	56	Nationwide Life* ...	846,565,697	-13.0
7	Aetna Life	4,584,187,521	-22.4	57	Life of Georgia	831,465,522	6.9
8	Conn. General	3,940,862,088	-34.2	58	Old Security, Mo. ...	803,458,864	3.0
9	Occidental Life, Calif.	3,714,357,810	17.5	59	Valley Forge Life ...	768,825,288	.6
10	Travelers	3,586,194,829	-36.8	60	Safeco Life	740,744,554	32.1
11	Lincoln National	3,277,353,735	-7.9	61	Life of No. America .	733,407,098	-1.0
12	Mass. Mutual*	2,769,857,434	6.2	62	ITT Hamilton, Mo. ..	723,819,907	28.7
13	Credit Life, Ohio ...	2,599,065,459	7.8	63	Farmers New World .	711,292,709	32.2
14	Northwestern Mutual*	2,439,871,968	19.0	64	National Life, Vt.* ..	691,887,472	10.5
15	State Farm Life	2,427,363,672	-8.1	65	Washington National	687,724,763	-11.1
16	Allstate Life	2,256,034,000	21.7	66	U.S. Life	681,714,575	20.0
17	National L&A	2,175,737,212	4.7	67	Durham Life	663,177,673	22.9
18	New England Life ...	2,164,800,551	4.5	68	Southwestern Life ...	636,522,863	-18.7
19	Minnesota Mutual* .	2,121,514,651	46.5	69	Combined Ins.	634,184,407	86.6
20	Sun Life, Canada* ...	2,078,261,854	12.5	70	Pilot Life	633,479,525	-5.2
21	Mutual of N.Y.*	2,058,232,061	-9.7	71	Union Mutual*	633,033,618	11.5
22	Crown Life, Canada*	2,010,380,000	21.7	72	Southern Farm Bur. .	618,314,827	13.8
23	American National ..	1,909,431,565	-12.4	73	American Gen., Del.	614,123,596	7.1
24	Phoenix Mutual	1,877,478,781	36.5	74	Liberty Life	613,581,804	.1
25	Republic National ...	1,842,826,802	47.5	75	Kentucky Central ...	612,770,607	.1
26	Mutual Benefit*	1,743,780,033	1.9	76	Fidelity Union	608,960,429	7.3
27	Great-West Life*	1,586,072,000	37.5	77	Stuyvesant Life	592,034,862	-24.4
28	Western & Southern*	1,552,618,461	2.8	78	Rock River Life, Ill. .	587,687,144	1190.4
29	Provident L&A	1,536,381,700	6.8	79	Provident Mutual* ..	573,632,392	-1.7
30	Conn. Mutual*	1,477,484,873	7.7	80	Southland Life	569,262,754	10.7
31	The Bankers Life* ...	1,469,718,627	10.6	81	Standard L&A*	568,814,983	5.3
32	United Benefit	1,429,385,076	36.2	82	Life of Virginia	558,137,772	-21.8
33	London Life, Canada	1,412,707,809	17.2	83	National Old Line* ..	555,656,309	56.4
34	Manufacturers Life ..	1,344,477,792	6.7	84	Life & Casualty*	545,916,858	12.3
35	Northwestern Nat. ..	1,260,673,944	12.6	85	American Bankers, Fla.	535,977,806	20.0
36	American United* ..	1,259,770,169	30.1	86	All Amer. L&C	532,626,772	24.6
37	Penn Mutual*	1,257,293,239	-1.0	87	National Fidelity	523,918,667	1.3
38	Franklin Life	1,255,393,598	3.4	88	American Defender .	510,750,192	23.4
39	Confederation Life* .	1,202,382,000	-20.0	89	Standard Ins., Ore. ..	505,419,682	51.6
40	Investors Syn. Life ..	1,161,472,839	23.1	90	Imperial Life, Canada*	497,653,000	-.8
41	Independent L&A ..	1,141,764,644	17.2	91	United Investors, Mo.	488,716,018	92.7
42	Canada Life*	1,140,835,000	26.3	92	Charter National, Mo.	486,996,530	2.0
43	Business Men's Assur.	1,126,239,561	9.3	93	Commonwealth Life	482,113,861	-6.8
44	Integon Life Corp. ..	1,110,130,257	13.0	94	Interstate L&A	481,238,361	5.1
45	Guardian Life*	1,102,393,359	10.4	95	Cherokee National .	463,541,417	1.9
46	Equity Funding	1,100,913,621	32.2	96	No. Am. Co. L&H ..	448,044,522	15.9
47	Mutual Life, Canada*	1,097,496,000	34.1	97	Union Security, Ga. .	441,815,642	57.6
48	Liberty National	1,077,197,354	2.1	98	Ford Life	439,903,525	12.8
49	Continental Assur. ..	1,075,578,192	-6.2	99	Old Line Life	436,700,613	3.1
50	United Ins.	1,020,347,251	54.9	100	Bankers L&C	436,198,481	40.6

The top 100 life-insurance
companies ranked by total assets

Rank 1971	Company	Assets in 1971	Rank 1970	% Incr. over 1970	$ Incr. over 1961	Rank 1961
1	Prudential*	$31,159,595,798	1	7.0	$13,586,168,798	2
2	Metropolitan Life*	29,163,289,584	2	4.7	10,395,875,584	1
3	Equitable Society*	15,395,252,785	3	7.1	4,959,181,785	3
4	New York Life*	11,268,290,241	4	4.9	3,798,162,241	4
5	John Hancock*	10,603,730,789	5	5.5	4,098,267,789	5
6	Aetna Life	7,803,598,009	6	8.2	3,477,569,009	7
7	Northwestern Mutual*	6,453,468,321	7	5.4	2,089,543,321	6
8	Conn. General	5,668,818,871	8	11.9	3,254,558,871	12
9	Travelers	5,043,962,470	9	7.1	1,567,835,470	8
10	Mass. Mutual*	4,566,073,943	10	6.5	1,962,073,943	10
11	Mutual Of N.Y.*	3,946,643,280	11	5.3	1,100,332,280	9
12	Sun Life, Canada*	3,874,400,242	12	5.8	1,393,484,242	11
13	New England Life*	3,751,747,039	13	5.9	1,421,427,039	13
14	Conn. Mutual*	2,922,383,340	14	5.8	1,203,861,340	16
15	Mutual Benefit*	2,697,999,472	15	5.0	768,255,472	14
16	Teachers Ins. & Ann.	2,596,517,000	17	14.3	1,815,923,000	32
17	Penn Mutual*	2,512,202,278	16	3.5	640,049,278	15
18	Lincoln National	2,363,641,503	18	5.0	769,905,503	17
19	The Bankers Life*	2,250,752,932	19	9.9	1,097,392,932	18
20	Manufacturers Life*	2,192,604,644	20	7.5	1,138,672,644	20
21	Western & Southern*	1,979,944,838	21	5.7	855,249,838	19
22	National L&A	1,890,467,549	22	6.5	930,861,549	21
23	Occidental Life, Calif.	1,796,042,020	23	6.6	897,528,020	25
24	Continental Assur.	1,769,560,711	25	8.6	952,904,711	29
25	London Life, Canada	1,734,262,029	24	6.3	863,170,029	27
26	Great-West*	1,634,455,888	26	7.1	780,068,888	28
27	National Life, Vt.*	1,521,937,919	27	5.9	638,956,919	26
28	American National	1,487,367,412	28	6.0	557,875,412	23
29	Phoenix Mutual*	1,446,621,813	29	4.8	503,693,813	22
30	Canada Life*	1,406,776,120	30	6.9	647,828,120	33
31	Franklin Life	1,311,253,003	31	6.7	666,792,003	37
32	State Mutual*	1,305,420,613	33	7.2	517,283,613	31
33	Mutual Life, Canada*	1,288,082,996	32	4.9	565,525,996	34
34	Provident Mutual*	1,190,955,065	34	3.9	291,933,065	24
35	Southwestern Life	1,122,483,680	35	7.4	489,068,680	39
36	Jefferson Standard	1,056,130,655	36	6.0	388,847,655	36
37	Guardian Life*	993,117,189	37	5.9	448,872,189	41
38	Pacific Mutual*	992,237,906	39	8.1	353,218,906	38
39	Equitable Life, Ia.	958,060,637	38	3.2	248,577,637	35
40	Confederation Life*	933,888,000	42	13.4	434,624,000	44
41	Union Central*	919,143,578	40	2.2	104,483,578	30
42	State Farm Life	902,200,633	45	14.6	660,647,633	63
43	Life of Virginia	894,793,348	41	5.4	342,457,348	40
44	Home Life, N.Y.*	884,518,739	43	8.1	436,704,739	45
45	Liberty National	864,926,200	44	8.4	513,589,200	54
46	Crown Life, Canada*	809,597,491	46	8.9	447,538,491	53
47	United Benefit	770,031,293	47	8.2	373,596,293	49
48	No. Amer. Life, Canada*	749,356,870	48	6.8	382,516,870	52
49	Provident L&A	717,980,343	50	13.5	476,727,343	66
50	Minnesota Mutual*	694,797,195	51	12.4	374,488,195	57

Rank 1971	Company	Assets in 1971	Rank 1970	% Incr. over 1970	$ Incr. over 1961	Rank 1961
51	Northwestern National	690,172,204	49	7.4	289,747,204	48
52	Mutual of Omaha*	625,093,250	54	9.9	339,608,283	43
53	General American*	607,133,282	55	10.8	311,386,282	60
54	Acacia Mutual*	596,172,965	53	3.5	171,461,965	46
55	Fidelity Mutual*	595,543,535	52	3.0	204,482,535	50
56	Nationwide Life	577,035,580	59	12.6	392,754,580	82
57	Washington National	569,383,923	57	6.1	245,995,923	56
58	Bankers L&C	567,200,771	62	15.3	359,729,771	78
59	Kansas City Life	555,196,254	56	2.7	134,257,254	47
60	Southland Life	553,106,049	58	6.7	234,172,049	58
61	Life & Casualty	538,859,041	60	5.7	205,098,041	55
62	Imperial Life, Canada*	533,423,222	61	6.5	221,885,222	59
63	Commonwealth Life	506,326,678	65	15.4	302,391,678	79
64	Country Life	489,598,795	63	8.1	270,917,795	75
65	Life of Georgia	480,251,704	64	8.6	255,210,704	72
66	Pilot Life	472,192,412	66	8.2	246,299,412	71
67	Calif.-Western States	458,553,618	68	8.2	189,227,618	61
68	United Ins.	456,487,040	69	11.2	309,463,040	90
69	Paul Revere	445,774,406	67	4.5	212,259,406	68
70	Monumental Life	417,456,491	70	5.2	159,331,491	62
71	Gulf Life	414,623,261	71	8.4	191,003,261	73
72	Republic National	411,507,068	89	48.4	297,310,068	106
73	American United	405,425,541	75	12.3	229,007,541	83
74	Business Men's Assur.	396,333,552	74	7.3	170,045,552	70
75	Ohio National*	394,185,546	72	5.3	162,201,546	69
76	Pan-Amer. Life*	394,039,895	73	5.5	153,873,895	87
77	Dominion Life, Canada*	378,107,234	76	6.1	165,293,234	76
78	Monarch Life	373,225,230	77	8.7	251,173,230	102
79	Bankers Life, Neb.*	370,463,832	79	9.0	215,163,832	88
80	Great Southern	363,477,441	78	6.1	122,179,441	66
81	Home Beneficial	348,399,739	81	7.4	175,956,739	84
82	Manhattan Life	344,321,580	80	4.6	148,291,580	80
83	Union Mutual*	336,888,596	83	9.8	207,859,439	63
84	Central Life, Ia.*	318,122,472	85	6.3	129,232,472	81
85	Lutheran Mutual*	314,445,862	88	9.5	184,596,862	97
86	American General, Del.	314,211,758	82	1.1	150,469,758	87
87	Berkshire Life*	311,039,512	84	2.6	98,554,512	77
88	Mutual Trust	303,082,884	86	3.8	84,036,884	74
89	Liberty Life	302,095,295	90	10.4	160,925,295	91
90	Transamerica Corp.	298,794,502	87	3.9	—	—
91	Life of No. Amer.	295,675,913	91	10.1	269,344,913	208
92	Southern Farm Bur.	290,975,142	97	16.1	239,786,142	155
93	Independent L&A	290,201,545	92	11.6	191,360,545	114
94	U.S. Life	283,333,655	105	29.3	157,738,655	99
95	Peoples Life, D.C.	279,777,702	94	8.9	127,397,702	89
96	Excelsior Life, Canada*	278,880,481	95	8.8	153,681,481	100
97	Allstate Life	277,028,336	104	25.9	251,485,336	211
98	Combined Ins.	276,184,752	103	25.0	242,706,307	50
99	Mass. Savings Bank*	271,539,249	93	5.1	99,144,249	85
100	Columbus Mutual*	270,413,352	96	7.4	103,135,352	86

The top 100 life-insurance companies
ranked by insurance in force

Rank 1971	Company	In Force in 1971	Rank 1970	% Incr. Over 1970	In Force in 1961	Rank 1961
1	Metropolitan Life*	$177,013,767,776	1	5.8	$98,006,726,000	1
2	Prudential*	168,252,643,385	2	7.3	85,666,687,000	2
3	Equitable Society*	82,777,097,685	3	7.6	41,656.798,000	3
4	John Hancock*	64,826,678,912	4	6.5	27,949,853,000	5
5	Aetna Life	62,907,282,314	5	5.0	25,732,663,000	6
6	Travelers	59,650,735,121	6	2.2	30,972,323,000	4
7	New York Life*	54,057,551,006	7	7.4	25,484,500,000	7
8	Conn. General	36,496,735,516	8	1.2	12,266,136,000	8
9	Occidental Life, Calif.	26,709,872,495	9	7.2	11,356,098,000	10
10	Lincoln National	22,767,938,805	10	4.1	11,454,190,000	9
11	Northwestern Mutual*	21,216,049,148	12	8.9	10,877,794,000	11
12	Mass Mutual*	20,906,604,154	11	6.6	8,984,585,000	13
13	Sun Life, Canada*	19,968,042,874	13	5.3	10,185,071,000	12
14	Cuna Mutual*	17,207,811,752	15	10.2	6,377,534,000	17
15	Mutual of N.Y.*	16,987,857,337	14	6.6	8,495,719,000	14
16	New England Life*	16,285,168,485	16	6.7	7,473,204,000	16
17	Continental Assur.	15,333,477,377	17	4.3	7,578,304,000	15
18	Mutual Benefit*	14,194,600,208	18	7.2	6,087,931,000	19
19	London Life, Canada*	12,424,465,689	19	8.2	6,004,094,000	21
20	Minnesota Mutual*	12,211,201,074	24	14.5	2,963,172,000	39
21	Provident L&A	11,682,518,130	23	9.4	3,534,886,000	30
22	Great West*	11,591,403,000	21	7.3	4,474,950,000	25
23	National L&A	11,553,296,239	22	7.4	6,117,140,000	18
24	Conn. Mutual*	11,338,190,345	25	8.1	5,039,030,000	24
25	State Farm Life	11,273,927,765	27	14.5	1,929,702,000	60
26	The Bankers Life*	11,264,882,472	26	9.6	3,973,752,000	28
27	Allstate Life	10,677,915,000	29	13.8	1,908,812,000	62
28	American National	10,469,493,933	20	–5.0	6,017,719,000	20
29	Western & Southern*	10,163,720,896	28	5.6	5,529,593,000	22
30	Manufacturers Life*	10,066,327,086	30	8.8	3,933,232,000	29
31	Republic National	10,019,695,671	39	36.7	3,261,467,000	35
32	Canada Life*	9,752,894,000	32	9.3	4,277,606,000	27
33	Penn Mutual*	9,606,781,479	31	5.3	5,503,393,000	23
34	Crown Life Canada*	9,405,164,000	33	17.2	3,025,210,000	37
35	Phoenix Mutual*	8,406,841,558	41	19.8	2,647,180,000	46
36	General American*	8,384,113,774	34	6.0	3,336,407,000	34
37	United Benefit	8,321,720,888	37	8.7	2,698,362,000	45
38	Confederation Life*	8,233,743,000	36	6.6	2,925,819,000	41
39	Franklin Life	8,181,996,151	35	3.8	4,429,292,000	26
40	State Mutual*	8,024,552,759	38	6.7	3,358,493,000	33
41	Mutual Life, Canada*	7,986,678,000	40	13.6	3,486,609,000	31
42	Northwestern National	7,116,655,567	43	14.2	2,529,812,000	48
43	Calif.-Western States	6,650,117,738	42	1.9	3,458,956,000	32
44	Home Life, N.Y.*	6,578,406,441	45	9.8	2,398.515.000	49
45	Life of Virginia	6,477,886,226	44	7.4	2,945,791,000	40
46	No. Amer. Life, Canada*	6,159,036,349	47	11.3	1,965,523,000	58
47	Guardian Life*	6,076,356,242	48	9.9	2,121,987,000	53
48	National Life, Vt.*	5,887,881,178	49	7.0	2,993,251,000	38
49	Provident Mutual*	5,823,146,631	50	6.7	2,787,602,000	43
50	Pilot Life	5,810,495,286	51	9.0	1,928,038,000	61

Rank 1971	Company	In Force in 1971	Rank 1970	% Incr. Over 1970	In Force in 1961	Rank 1961
51	Business Men's Assur.	5,732,417,709	53	8.3	2,225,671,000	50
52	Nationwide Life	5,724,380,560	54	8.4	2,033,893,000	57
53	Pacific Mutual*	5,666,552,969	46	.8	2,833,840,000	42
54	Old Republic Life	5,660,655,293	52	6.2	2,624,317,000	47
55	Southwestern Life	5,565,091,640	55	6.9	2,710,233,000	44
56	American United*	5,532,283,073	57	9.3	1.775,994,000	67
57	Liberty National	5,500,054,449	56	6.5	2,203,233,000	51
58	Washington National	5,297,308,526	58	9.6	2,123,909,000	52
59	North Amer. Re.	5,111,762,137	59	11.1	1,538,934,000	69
60	Life of North Amer.	5,001,005,003	60	10.1	866,518,000	97
61	Union Mutual*	4,692,917,670	61	9.7	1,144,250,000	73
62	U.S. Life	4,263,244,010	74	39.5	1,827,762,000	66
63	Union Central*	4,194,664,194	62	.5	3,171,171,000	36
64	Life & Casualty	4,008,933,819	64	5.0	2,064,945,000	56
65	Investors Synd. Life	3,974,642,647	71	19.3	562,870,000	130
66	Jefferson Standard	3,963,277,954	63	3.8	2,103,918,000	55
67	Life of Georgia	3,924,378,570	66	8.6	1,863,512,000	64
68	Southland Life	3,891,593,352	65	5.1	1,880,834,000	63
69	Commonwealth Life	3,806,555,998	69	12.7	1,532,235,000	70
70	Integon Life Corp.	3,447,198,366	72	6.4	1,375,323,000	76
71	Pan-Amer. Life*	3,443,022,972	68	.3	1,457,614,000	71
72	North Amer. L&C	3,422,407,453	67	−5.1	1,155,497,000	82
73	Gulf Life	3,414,034,819	73	6.2	1,417,369,000	74
74	American H&L	3,343,411,371	79	16.8	1,152,962,000	83
75	League Life	3,257,280,130	70	−2.5	211,775,000	224
76	Imperial Life, Canada*	3,216,137,000	76	7.8	1,302,844,000	77
77	American General, Del.	3,196,409,635	75	6.2	927,120,000	93
78	Liberty Life	3,161,781,693	78	7.9	1,394,631,000	75
79	Standard Ins., Ore.	3,153,659,261	84	19.0	870,207,000	96
80	Fidelity Union	3,110,556,039	80	9.3	601,307,000	123
81	Acacia Mutual*	3,057,414,402	77	3.4	1,943,575,000	59
82	Security Benefit*	3,049,378,452	96	26.2	545,402,000	136
83	Credit Life, Ohio	3,031,941,297	81	8.9	1,227,618,000	79
84	Southern Farm Bur.	2,972,518,255	85	14.2	671,519,000	115
85	Farmers New World	2,935,325,461	92	17.5	492,250,000	146
86	Safeco Life	2,880,124,840	100	23.0	212,685,000	223
87	N.Y. Savings Bank*	2,865,848,885	94	15.7	498,394,000	145
88	Equitable Life, Ia.	2,856,659,713	82	5.3	1,841,420,000	65
89	United Ins.	2,783,896,724	115	38.1	853,385,000	98
90	Hartford Life	2,758,622,721	83	2.7	893,341,000	94
91	Bankers Life, Neb.*	2,751,538,693	89	8.5	890,020,000	95
92	National Life, Canada*	2,739,728,107	99	15.9	550,386,000	133
93	Monumental Life	2,702,824,276	87	5.5	1,220,907,000	80
94	Paul Revere	2,696,754,027	97	12.2	1,003,752,000	91
95	Fidelity Mutual*	2,684,770,789	86	3.6	1,379,292,000	76
96	Protective Life	2,659,512,360	102	15.6	1,187,940,000	81
97	American-Amicable	2,621,233,800	90	3.7	573,744,000	129
98	Union Labor Life	2,596,653,913	88	1.6	1,147,743,000	84
99	Kansas City Life	2,579,602,131	95	6.8	1,417,932,000	73
100	Teachers Ins. & Ann.	2,577,073,394	98	7.8	602,755,000	122

A "SPECIMEN" LIFE-INSURANCE POLICY

Below begins an example of how a life-insurance policy might look. There being no such thing as a "standard" policy, this was adapted from one prepared by the Institute of Life Insurance, an industry organization, for training and teaching purposes.

THE INSTITUTE LIFE INSURANCE COMPANY

The Company WILL PAY the Face Amount to the Beneficiary upon receipt of due proof of the Insured's death, subject to the provisions on the following pages of this policy.

Policy Number	**SPECIMEN**	Insured	*Thomas A. Benson*
Face Amount	$10,000	Date of Issue	May 1, 1972

Signed at the Home Office of The Institute Life Insurance Company, 93 Fifth Avenue, New York, New York 10010 — on the date of issue.

Albert S. Bright, *President*   John H. Sloan, *Secretary*

SPECIFICATIONS

INSURED	THOMAS A. BENSON			
POLICY NUMBER	**SPECIMEN**		$10,000	**FACE AMOUNT**
BENEFICIARY	HELEN M. BENSON		5-1-1972	**POLICY DATE**
RELATIONSHIP	WIFE			
ISSUE AGE	35	STANDARD CLASS	5-1-1972	**DATE OF ISSUE**

—SCHEDULE OF BENEFITS AND PREMIUMS—

ANNUAL PREMIUM
$227.90

BASIC BENEFIT — LIFE INSURANCE

ADDITIONAL BENEFITS — AS PROVIDED BY RIDER

BENEFIT		ANNUAL PREMIUM
ACCIDENTAL DEATH	FOR BASIC BENEFIT	$8.50 FOR 35 YEARS
WAIVER OF PREMIUM	FOR BASIC BENEFIT	$6.20 FOR 30 YEARS

PREMIUM AMOUNTS AND DUE DATES — The Premium for the policy consists of the sum of the applicable annual premiums shown above. The amount of the first premium is $242.60.

DUE DATES OF 2ND AND LATER PREMIUMS — at 12 policy month intervals after the policy date.

A BRIEF DESCRIPTION OF THIS POLICY

This is a WHOLE LIFE POLICY. Insurance is payable in event of death. Annual dividends. Premiums are payable for life unless the Policy is previously paid-up by dividends.

DEATH PROCEEDS

The proceeds payable at the death of the Insured shall be (a) the amount of any insurance then in force on his life, including any provided by additional benefit rider or endorsement, or by dividends, plus (b) any existing dividend deposits and any dividend that the Company may grant and credit in cash at the Insured's death, plus (c) if the Insured dies while the Policy is in force on a premium-paying basis, and if the last premium was not waived under any provision for waiver of premiums, that part of the last premium as was paid for the part of the premium interval which extends beyond the policy month in which the Insured dies, less (d) any indebtedness to the Company on this Policy and less (e) if the Insured dies during the grace period of an overdue premium, an amount equal to one month's premium. Payment, in any case, will be subject to all of the provisions of this Policy.

BENEFICIARY

DETERMINATION OF BENEFICIARY — The beneficiary is as designated in the application for this Policy and in the specifications page unless otherwise provided by endorsement at issue or unless subsequently changed as provided below.

Any reference in any beneficiary designation to a beneficiary living or surviving shall, unless otherwise provided, mean living on the earlier of (a) the day due proof of the Insured's death is received by the Company at its Home Office and (b) the 14th day after the Insured's death. The share of the death proceeds of any beneficiary who is not living on such earlier day will be payable to the remaining beneficiaries in the manner provided in such beneficiary designation. If no beneficiary is then living and unless otherwise provided, the death proceeds will be payable to the Insured's executors or administrators.

CHANGE OF BENEFICIARY — Beneficiary changes may be made during the Insured's lifetime by written notice to the Company at its Home Office, but the Policy need not be presented for endorsement unless required by the Company. Any change shall take effect as of the date the notice was signed, upon acceptance and recording at the Home Office, subject to any payment made by the Company or action taken by it before receipt of the notice at the Home Office.

RIGHTS

During the Insured's lifetime, all rights under this Policy belong exclusively as designated in the application for this Policy unless otherwise provided by endorsement. Such rights include the right to change the beneficiary, to assign, and all other rights, benefits, options, and privileges conferred by this Policy o allowed by the Company.

DIVIDENDS

ANNUAL DIVIDENDS — While this policy is in force except as extended term insurance, the share of the divisible surplus accruing on this Policy shall be determined by the Company and allotted as a dividend at the end of the second and of each later policy year.

Each dividend may be applied under one of the options below. Option 1 shall be automatic unless another is elected not later than 3 months after the date of allotment.

1. Dividend Addition — Applied as paid-up additional insurance on the Insured's life.

2. Cash — Paid in cash.

3. Premium Payment — Applied toward payment of a premium if the remainder is paid by the end of the grace period.

4. Dividend Deposit — Left on deposit with the Company. Interest shall be added on each policy anniversary at the rate determined by the Company for each year, but never less than 2½%, and shall become part of the amount on deposit.

Any dividend allotted while this Policy is continued as reduced paid-up life insurance after default in premium payment shall be applied as a dividend addition.

CASH VALUE OF DIVIDENDS — Any existing additions and deposits not required as security for a loan may be surrendered for their cash value at any time during the Insured's lifetime. The cash value of additions shall be their present value but never less than the original dividends applied as such additions. The cash value of deposits shall be the amount on deposit.

POLICY PAID-UP BY DIVIDENDS — If at any time the cash value of existing additions and deposits equals the then present value of future net premiums, the Company will, upon written request, apply such cash value to continue this Policy in force without further premium payments.

PREMIUM PAYMENTS AND GRACE PERIOD

Premiums after the first are payable on each due date specified on page 3 occurring before the end of the premium period, which shall be reckoned from the Policy Date. No premium is payable *if its due date is on or after the date of the Insured's death.*

Each such premium is payable to the Company, either at its Home Office or elsewhere, through any agent or other person authorized by the Company to collect premiums, but only in exchange for a receipt signed by the Treasurer of the Company and by the person receiving the premium.

If any premium after the first is not paid on or before its due date, or within a grace period of 31 days thereafter, during which period this Policy shall continue in force, this Policy shall immediately terminate and have no further value except as may be provided under "Optional Benefits on Lapse".

SETTLEMENT OPTIONS

Death proceeds payable under this Policy, or endowment or surrender proceeds, if any, may be settled under one of the following options instead of being paid in one sum, provided (a) the proceeds are at least $1,000 and are payable to a natural person in his own right and (b) the payments under the option elected are also to be payable to such person (referred to below as the payee).

1. INTEREST INCOME—The Company will hold the proceeds as principal and will pay interest during the payee's lifetime. Interest will be at the rate determined by the Company for each year, but never less than $2\frac{3}{4}\%$ a year.

2. INCOME FOR SPECIFIED PERIOD — The Company will pay an income for the number of years elected, in accordance with this table showing the monthly income for each $1,000 of proceeds. Payments may be increased by additional interest as determined by the Company for each year.

Years	1	2	3	4	5	6	7	8	9	10
Amount	$84.37	42.76	28.89	21.96	17.80	15.03	13.06	11.58	10.42	9.50
Years	11	12	13	14	15	16	17	18	19	20
Amount	$8.75	8.13	7.60	7.15	6.76	6.41	6.11	5.85	5.61	5.39

3. SINGLE LIFE INCOME — The Company will pay an income during the period certain elected and during the payee's remaining lifetime. The period certain elected may be (a) 0 years or (b) 10 years or (c) 20 years or (d) the period required for the total income payments to equal the proceeds (refund period certain). The income will be in the amount determined by the Company on the date the proceeds become payable, but not less than the minimum amount shown, for the period certain elected, in accordance with the Option 3 table.

OPTION 3 — MINIMUM MONTHLY INCOME FOR EACH $1,000 OF PROCEEDS

The life income shown is based on the payee's age at nearest birthday on the due date of the first income payment.

AGE	0 Years Certain	10 Years Certain	20 Years Certain	Refund Period Certain	AGE	0 Years Certain	10 Years Certain	20 Years Certain	Refund Period Certain
				MALE PAYEE					
10	$2.69	$2.69	$2.69	$2.68	50	$ 4.39	$4.32	$4.12	$ 4.11
15	2.77	2.77	2.77	2.76	55	4.95	4.83	4.46	4.53
20	2.87	2.87	2.87	2.85	60	5.70	5.45	4.80	5.07
25	3.00	3.00	2.99	2.97	65	6.73	6.26	5.10	5.76
30	3.16	3.15	3.14	3.12	70	8.22	7.16	5.29	6.69
35	3.36	3.35	3.32	3.29	75	10.40	8.11	5.37	7.94
40	3.62	3.60	3.54	3.51	80	13.66	8.89	5.39	9.65
45	3.95	3.92	3.81	3.78	85	18.65	9.32	5.39	12.04
				FEMALE PAYEE					
10*	$2.63	$2.63	$2.63	$2.62	50	$ 3.96	$3.94	$3.85	$ 3.83
15	2.70	2.70	2.70	2.69	55	4.41	4.36	4.19	4.19
20	2.78	2.78	2.78	2.77	60	5.02	4.92	4.57	4.66
25	2.89	2.89	2.88	2.87	65	5.88	5.65	4.94	5.29
30	3.01	3.01	3.00	2.99	70	7.12	6.56	5.22	5.12
35	3.17	3.17	3.15	3.13	75	8.98	7.62	5.35	7.26
40	3.37	3.36	3.34	3.32	80	11.84	8.60	5.39	8.85
45	3.63	3.61	3.57	3.54	85†	16.36	9.22	5.39	11.11

3A. JOINT LIFE INCOME (Available only for endowment or surrender proceeds, if any) — The Company will pay a joint and survivor income, of the type elected, during the joint lifetime of the payee and another person, one of whom must be the Insured, and during the survivor's remaining lifetime. The type elected may provide a survivor's income equal to (a) the amount payable during the joint lifetime or (b) two-thirds of the amount payable during the joint lifetime. The income payable during the joint lifetime will be in the amount determined by the Company on the date the proceeds become payable, but not less than the minimum amount applicable, for the type of joint and survivor income elected, in accordance with the Option 3A table.

OPTION 3A — MINIMUM MONTHLY INCOME FOR EACH $1,000 OF PROCEEDS

The income shown is based on the ages (at nearest birthday on the due date of the first income payment) of the 2 persons during whose joint lifetime payments are to be made.

SAME INCOME CONTINUED TO SURVIVOR						TWO-THIRDS OF INCOME CONTINUED TO SURVIVOR				
AGE OF FEMALE	AGE OF MALE					AGE OF FEMALE	AGE OF MALE			
	50	55	60	65	70		50	55	60	65	70
50	$3.67	$3.77	$3.84	$3.89	$3.92	50	$3.99	$4.17	$4.36	$4.56	$4.77
55	3.86	4.02	4.15	4.24	4.32	55	4.20	4.43	4.66	4.91	5.17
60	4.03	4.27	4.48	4.67	4.80	60	4.44	4.72	5.02	5.34	5.67
65	4.16	4.49	4.82	5.13	5.40	65	4.70	5.05	5.43	5.84	6.29
70	4.26	4.67	5.12	5.60	6.06	70	4.98	5.39	5.87	6.42	7.02

4. INCOME OF SPECIFIED AMOUNT — The Company will pay an income of the amount elected, but not less each year than 7% of the proceeds, as long as the proceeds and interest last. Interest will be credited annually on the remaining proceeds at the rate determined by the Company for each year, but never less than 2¾%.

OTHER SETTLEMENT OPTIONS — The proceeds may be settled under any option not specified above that may be agreed to by the Company.

ELECTION OF SETTLEMENT — During the Insured's lifetime, one of the above options may be elected for proceeds payable by reason of his death, or a previous election changed, subject to the same conditions and effective in the same manner as a change of beneficiary.

The payee of any proceeds may elect one of these options within 1 month after the proceeds become payable provided the proceeds are payable in one sum and have not yet been paid. Election must be made by written notice to the Company at its Home Office.

PAYMENT PROVISIONS — A supplementary contract providing for the settlement will be issued when the proceeds are settled under one of these options. The date of the supplementary contract shall be the date of the Insured's death if the proceeds settled are death proceeds and the settlement was elected during the Insured's lifetime. Otherwise the supplementary contract shall bear the date the proceeds become payable.

Payments will be made monthly unless quarterly, semi-annual, or annual payments are requested in the election. However, if the payments elected would be less than $10 each, payments on a less frequent basis may be made at the Company's option.

To obtain the amount of other than monthly payments, multiply the monthly payment by the appropriate factor.	Annual	Semi-Annual	Quarterly
Option 2	$11.85	$5.97	$2.99
Option 3—0 Years Certain	11.68	5.90	2.97
Option 3—20 Years Certain, or Refund Period Certain	11.80	5.95	2.99
Option 3—10 Years Certain, or OPTION 3A	11.74	5.92	2.97

The first payment under Option 2, 3, 3A, or 4 will be due as of the date of the supplementary contract. The first payment under Option 1 will be due 1, 3, 6, or 12 months after such date, depending on whether payments are monthly, quarterly, semi-annual, or annual.

Before making payment under Option 3 or 3A, the Company will require evidence satisfactory to it of the age of the person or persons during whose lifetime payments are to be made.

After the date of the supplementary contract, the settlement cannot be modified or terminated before all payments required by its terms have been made, except as provided below and except as approved by the Company at the time of election of the settlement and upon such terms as it shall then consider necessary.

At the payee's death, any settlement under Option 1, 2, 3, or 4 will terminate. Any amount specified below for that option will be paid in one sum to the payee's executors or administrators, unless otherwise elected within such limitations as the Company shall consider necessary.

Option 1 — The principal with any interest to date of death.

Option 2 — The commuted value, based on interest at 2¾% a year, compounded annually, of any future income payments for the specified period.

Option 3 — The commuted value, based on interest at the rate or rates assumed in computing the amount of income, compounded annually, of any future income payments for the specified period certain.

Option 4 — The unpaid proceeds and interest to date of death.

GENERAL PROVISIONS

THE CONTRACT — This Policy has been issued in consideration of the application and of the payment of premiums as provided. The Policy and the application (copy of which is attached and made a part of the Policy) constitute the entire contract.

STATEMENTS IN APPLICATION — All statements made in the application shall be deemed representations and not warranties. No such statements shall invalidate this Policy or be used in defense to a claim under the Policy, unless contained in the written application and unless a copy of the application is attached to this Policy when issued.

DATES AND POLICY PERIODS — Where dates are shown the numerals represent month-day-year, in that order. Years, months, and anniversaries are reckoned from the Policy Date, unless otherwise indicated. Each policy month begins on the same date in each calendar month as that specified in the Policy Date (when there is no same date, on the last day of the calendar month).

INCONTESTABILITY — This Policy shall be incontestable after it has been in force during the lifetime of the Insured for 2 years from its date of issue, except for non-payment of premiums and except as to any provision for waiver of premiums.

MISSTATEMENT OF AGE — If the Insured's age has been misstated, any amount payable by the Company at any time shall be such as the premium would have purchased at the correct age.

SUICIDE — In event of the suicide of the Insured within 2 years after the date of issue, the amount payable by the Company shall be limited to the amount of the premiums paid.

PREMIUM INTERVAL CHANGE — The interval of payment for future premiums may be changed to annual, semi-annual, or quarterly, in accordance with the premium schedule in effect at the date of issue, provided the resulting premium amount and due dates are satisfactory to the Company.

Any such change shall be effective upon acceptance by the Company of payment of the premium for the new interval or upon receipt by the Company of written request for such change.

ASSIGNMENT — The Company shall not be charged with notice of any assignment of any interest in this Policy until the original assignment or a certified copy has been filed with the Company at its Home Office.

The Company assumes no responsibility as to the validity or effect of any assignment and may rely solely on the assignee's statement as to the amount of his interest. All assignments shall be subject to any indebtedness to the Company on this Policy.

The interest of any beneficiary or other person shall be subordinate to any assignment, regardless of when the assignment was made, and the assignee shall receive any sum payable to the extent of his interest.

POLICY PAYMENT — All sums payable by the Company are payable at its Home Office. In any settlement of this Policy, the Company may require return of this Policy.

Due proof of death or disability must be submitted to the Company at its Home Office on forms furnished by it.

RELATIONSHIPS — Relationships used in any beneficiary or other designation shall refer to the Insured unless the wording of the designation indicates otherwise.

AUTHORITY — No agent or other person, except the President, a Vice-President, or a Secretary of the Company, has authority to accept any representations or information not contained in the written application for this Policy, or to modify or enlarge this contract, or to waive any requirement in this contract.

CASH VALUE

This Policy may be surrendered at any time for its cash value less any indebtedness. Cash values on certain policy anniversaries, assuming no default in premium payment, are shown for each $1,000 of face amount in the table on page 186. The method of determining those values, and the values at other times, before and after default, is explained below.

METHOD OF DETERMINING CASH VALUE—If all past due premiums have been paid, the cash value of this Policy is the cash value of the face amount plus the cash value of any existing dividend additions or deposits. The cash value of the face amount on any policy anniversary is computed by the Standard Nonforfeiture Value Method, with the nonforfeiture factors shown on page 186. The cash value of the face amount at any other time during a policy year shall be determined by the Company, with allowance for the time that has elapsed in that year and for any premium paid for that year.

A detailed statement of the method of determining cash values has been filed with the insurance supervisory official of the state or province in which this Policy is delivered.

If any past due premium is unpaid, the cash value of this Policy is as follows:

(a) Within 60 days after the due date of the premium first in default, the cash value is the same as on that due date, less the cash value of any dividend additions and deposits surrendered after such due date.

(b) After such 60 days, if this Policy is continued as reduced paid-up life or extended term insurance, the cash value at any time is the then present value of the amount of insurance in force. However, while such insurance is in force during the 30 days after any policy anniversary, the cash value shall not be less than on the anniversary.

DEFINITIONS — Cash values computed by the Standard Nonforfeiture Value Method are equivalent to the present value of the guaranteed life insurance benefit less the present value of the applicable nonforfeiture factors for each year remaining in the premium period. The values (other than monthly incomes) in the values table and net premiums and present values referred to in this Policy are based on the Commissioners 1958 Standard Ordinary Mortality Table (except that net single premiums and present values in connection with extended term insurance are based on the Commissioners 1958 Extended Term Insurance Table), assuming continuous functions and interest at 2½% a year. Any additional benefits provided by rider or endorsement are disregarded in determining the cash value of this Policy. Net single premiums referred to under "Optional Benefits on Lapse" shall be those at the Insured's age (at nearest birthday) on the policy anniversary nearest the date as of which they are applied. They shall be applied as of the due date of the premium first in default.

LOANS

Loans may be obtained from the Company at any time while this Policy has a cash value except during any period of extended term insurance.

The loan value in the amount which, with interest at 5% a year, shall equal the cash value of this Policy on the next policy anniversary or, in the case of an automatic premium loan, on the next premium due date if that is earlier.

CASH LOAN — A loan for any amount not exceeding the loan value will be made upon proper assignment of this Policy to the Company. If required by the Company, any or all unpaid premiums due before the next policy anniversary and any existing indebtedness shall be paid out of any loan.

AUTOMATIC LOAN TO PAY PREMIUMS (Subject to conditions specified below) — This provision shall become operative if requested in the application for this Policy or whenever written request is received by the Company at its Home Office before any premium is in default beyond the grace period. It shall become inoperative, as to premiums not yet paid, upon (a) receipt by the Company at its Home Office of written request to that effect or (b) election of an Optional Benefit on Lapse within the grace period.

While this provision is operative and the loan value is at least as great as the total unpaid premium plus any existing indebtedness, each premium for this Policy due and not otherwise paid will be paid by automatic loan on the last day of the grace period. However, a premium shall not be paid by automatic loan if all premiums due during the twelve policy month interval prior to the due date of such premium have been paid by automatic loan and no payment toward indebtedness under this Policy has been made during such interval or during the grace period of such premium.

MISCELLANEOUS PROVISIONS — This Policy shall be the sole security for any loan but need not be presented for endorsement unless required by the Company.

Loan interest at 5% a year shall be payable on each policy anniversary and shall accrue from day to day between anniversaries. Any interest not paid when due shall be added to the loan and shall bear interest at the same rate.

If at any time the indebtedness equals or exceeds the cash value, this Policy shall terminate and have no further value, provided at least 31 days prior notice shall have been mailed to the last known address of the Insured and of any assignee of record.

Any indebtedness not otherwise repaid under the policy provisions may be repaid in whole or part before the Insured's death.

Indebtedness, wherever referred to, includes any loan interest due or accrued, as well as total loan principal under this Policy.

OPTIONAL BENEFITS ON LAPSE

If any premium due while this Policy has a cash value is not paid by the end of the grace period by automatic loan or otherwise, either A or B below shall immediately apply:

A. If this Policy is designated as Standard Class, it shall continue from the due date of the premium first in default as paid-up non-participating extended term insurance unless, within 60 days after such due date, it is surrendered for its cash value less any indebtedness or election is made to continue the Policy as reduced paid-up participating life insurance. The amount of extended term insurance shall be the face amount plus any existing dividend additions and deposits, less any indebtedness. Its period shall be such as the cash value less any indebtedness shall provide when applied as a net single premium. The amount of reduced paid-up life insurance shall be such as the cash value less any indebtedness shall provide when applied as a net single premium.

B. If this Policy is designated as Special Class, it shall continue as reduced paid-up participating life insurance unless it is surrendered for its cash value less any indebtedness. The amount of reduced paid-up life insurance shall be such as the cash value less any indebtedness shall provide when applied as a net single premium.

REINSTATEMENT

If any premium is not paid by the end of the grace period, and if this Policy has not been surrendered for cash, it may be reinstated at any time within 5 years after the due date of the premium first in default upon (1) evidence satisfactory to the Company of the Insured's insurability and (2) payment of all overdue premiums and payment or reinstatement of any indebtedness to the Company, together with payment of compound interest on such premiums and indebtedness at 5% a year.

POLICY CHANGES

This Policy may be changed to another form, kind, amount, or plan of insurance, subject to approval by the Company and to payment of such cost and furnishing of such requirements as it shall consider necessary.

TABLE OF CASH, LOAN, AND OTHER VALUES

(The extended term insurance option on lapse is available only if this Policy is designated as Standard Class.)

Values on the anniversaries indicated assume that all premiums up to such anniversaries have been paid and that there are no dividends or indebtedness. Values at other times will be furnished on request.

Cash and loan values, paid-up insurance, and nonforfeiture factors shown are for each $1,000 face amount. Monthly income amounts are minimum amounts and assume settlement of the cash value at the anniversary indicated under Settlement Option 3 with a 10 year period certain, on the Insured's life, in accordance with and subject to the provisions on pages 180 and 182. M means male and F, female. The period of extended term insurance is the same for any face amount.

The values are as great as or greater than the minimum values required by the law of the state or province in which the Policy is delivered.

Payment of the cash surrender value of this Policy or the making of any loan, other than a loan to pay premiums on policies in this Company, may be deferred by the Company for not more than 6 months after the application therefor is received by the Company at its Home Office. If payment of the cash surrender value is deferred for 30 days or more, the Company will pay interest at 2½% a year from the date of surrender to the date of payment.

Policy Anni-versary	Age on Anni-versary	EACH $1000 FACE CASH OR LOAN VALUE	PAID-UP LIFE INSURANCE	EXTENDED TERM INSURANCE (Available only if Policy is designated as Standard Class) YEARS	DAYS
1	36	—	—	—	—
2	37	$ 8	$ 19	2	61
3	38	27	60	6	34
4	39	46	100	8	311
5	40	65	138	10	311
10	45	166	317	15	319
15	50	265	459	16	297
20	55	361	571	16	60
27	62	493	696	14	130
30	65	548	741	13	175

MONTHLY INCOME

20	55	$1.74 M	$1.57 F
27	62	$2.83 M	$2.56 F
30	65	$3.43 M	$3.10 F

NONFORFEITURE FACTOR:

(EACH $1000 FACE— Used in computing cash values)	POLICY YEARS	FACTOR
	1–12	21.131
	13 & LATER	18.278

WHOLE LIFE AGE 35

Life Insurance Application To *The* **INSTITUTE** *Life Insurance Company* **New York**
PART I

IMPORTANT NOTICE—Be sure all questions in all parts of the application are answered completely and accurately, since the application is the basis of the insurance contract and will become part of any policy issued.

1. Insured's Full Name (Give title as Mr., Dr., Rev., Hon., etc.)	Sex

2. Single ☐   Married ☐   Widowed ☐   Divorced ☐   Separated ☐

3. Ins. Age	Date of Birth Mo.-Day-Yr.	Place of Birth	Social Sec. No.

4. Addresses last 5 yrs.   (St.-City-State-Zip Code-County)   Yrs.
Home: Present

    Former

Busi-   Present
ness:

    Former

Mail to: Home ☐   Business ☐

5. a) Occupations last 5 yrs.   Describe Exact Duties   Yrs.
    Present

    Former

    b) Employer

    c) Any change contemplated? Yes ☐   No ☐

6. Total Life Insurance in Force $	None ☐

	Yes	No
7. Have you ever been rejected, deferred or discharged by the Armed Forces for medical reasons or applied for a government disability rating?	☐	☐
8. a) In the past 3 years have you ever: 1. Operated, been a crew member of, or had any duties aboard any kind of aircraft?	☐	☐
2. Engaged in underwater diving below 40 feet, parachuting, auto or motorcycle racing, or other hazardous activities?	☐	☐
3. Had your driver's license suspended or revoked or been charged with more than one speeding violation?	☐	☐
b) In the future, do you intend to engage in any activities mentioned in 1 and 2 of a) above? (If "Yes" to any of 7 or 8 complete Supplemental Form)	☐	☐
9. Will coverage applied for replace any life insurance?	☐	☐
10. Are any other applications pending or contemplated?	☐	☐
11. Has an application for insurance or reinstatement ever been declined, postponed, modified or rated?	☐	☐
12. Do you intend going to a foreign country?	☐	☐

13. Face Amount $ Plan

    Accidental Death ☐   Applicant's W.P.   ☐

    Children's Term ☐   .... ☐

    Purchase Option ☐   .... ☐

    .... units of Wife's Term on wife, ...

    $............................. initial amt. Decreasing Term .... years

                (Joint ☐) (Mort. Pro. ☐) (Straight-Line ☐)

            Note: Waiver of Premium automatically included on qualified issues

14. Auto. Prem. Loan provision operative if available?   Yes ☐   No ☐

15. Divi-   Additions (for other than term)   ☐

    dend   Reduce premium, if applicable, otherwise cash   ☐

    Option   Deposits ☐   One Year Term ☐

                Supplemental Protection (Keyman Policy only)   ☐

16. Beneficiary—*For children's, wife's or joint insurance as provided in contract; for other insurance as follows, subject to policy's beneficiary provisions:*

                Name and Relationship to Insured

	(Name)	**(Relationship)**	
1st			if living, if not
2nd			if living, if not
3rd			if living, if not

the executors or administrators of:

    Insured ☐   Other (Specify in **Remarks**) ☐

    Joint beneficiaries will receive equally or survivor, unless otherwise specified.

17. Rights—During Insured's lifetime all rights belong to:

    Insured ☐   Other (Specify in **Remarks**) ☐

    (After Insured's death as provided in contract on wife's insurance.)

18. Premium Frequency ....   Amount Paid $...................

REMARKS [Include details (company, date, amt., etc.) for all questions 5c, 9, 10, 11 and 12 answered Yes]

I agree that: (1) No one but the Company's President, a Vice-President or Secretary has authority to accept information not contained in the application, to modify or enlarge any contract, or to waive any requirement. (2) Except as otherwise provided in any conditional receipt issued, any policy issued shall take effect upon its delivery and payment of the first premium during the lifetime of each person to be insured. Due dates of later premiums shall be as specified in the policy.

Dated at...on........................19....

                                  Signature

Countersigned by.......................................of Insured...........................

           Field Underwriter (Licensed Resident Agent)

Signature of Applicant (if other than Insured) who agrees to be bound by the representations and agreements in this and any other part of this application ....

             (Relationship)   (Address of Applicant)

INDEX